ASSESSING
ASSESSMENT

ASSESSING ACHIEVEMENT IN THE ARTS

ASSESSING ASSESSMENT

Series Editor:
Harry Torrance, University of Sussex

The aim of this series is to take a longer term view of current developments in assessment and to interrogate them in terms of research evidence deriving from both theoretical and empirical work. The intention is to provide a basis for testing the rhetoric of current policy and for the development of well-founded practice.

Current titles

Christopher Pole: *Assessing and Recording Achievement*
Malcolm Ross *et al.*: *Assessing Achievement in the Arts*

ASSESSING ACHIEVEMENT IN THE ARTS

Malcolm Ross, Hilary Radnor,
Sally Mitchell and Cathy Bierton

Open University Press
Buckingham · Philadelphia

Open University Press
Celtic Court
22 Ballmoor
Buckingham
MK18 1XW

and
1900 Frost Road, Suite 101
Bristol, PA 19007, USA

First Published 1993

A catalogue record of this book is available from the British Library

Library of Congress Cataloging-in-Publication Data
Assessing achievement in the arts/Malcolm Ross . . . [et al.].
    p.   cm.
  "A Leverhulme project."
  Includes bibliographical references.
  ISBN 0–335–19062–6 (hb.).—ISBN 0–335–19061–8 (pbk.)
  1. Arts—Study and teaching (Secondary)—Great Britain.
2. Academic achievement—Great Britain—Evaluation. 3. Teacher-
student relationships—Great Britain—Evaluation. I. Ross,
Malcolm, 1932–   .
NX343.A88   1993
700′.71′241—dc20   92–31892
                                                        CIP

Typeset by Colset Pte Ltd, Singapore
Printed in Great Britain by Biddles Ltd, Guildford and Kings Lynn

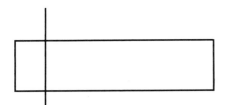

CONTENTS

Series editor's introduction		vii
Preface		x
Acknowledgements		xiv
1	**Contextualizing the project**	1
	The arts in education	1
	The assessment context	9
2	**The project's history**	19
	Research methods	19
	Phase 1	20
	Phase 2	26
	Phase 3	34
	Phase 4	47
	Writing up	48
3	**Theoretical**	50
	The arts curriculum cycle	50
	Another way of looking	57
4	**Case studies**	67
	Introduction	67
	Case study 1: The Harmonious Potter	70

Case study 2: Marching Orders   82
Case study 3: Catching Words   90
Case study 4: Seeing the Light   100
Case study 5: Making a Long Face   105
Case study 6: Joining the Dance   130
Case study 7: Talking Picture   145

5 Conclusion   157

Notes   170
References and bibliography   171
Index   174

SERIES EDITOR'S INTRODUCTION

Changing theories and methods of assessment have been the focus of significant attention for some years now, both in the UK and elsewhere. Within the UK increasing concerns over the validity and pedagogical implications of assessment have led to a number of developments, usually involving an increasing role for the teacher in school-based assessment. These developments carry many potentially beneficial consequences for the interrelation of teaching, learning and assessment, but they have also been introduced within an at best equivocal and at worst hostile political climate such that debates about accountability and the role of results in the educational marketplace have come to overshadow many of the educational issues.

It is precisely because of this complexity and confusion that the present series of books on assessment has been developed. Many claims are being made with respect to the efficacy of new approaches to assessment, which require careful review and investigation. Likewise, many changes are being required by government intervention, which may lead to hurried and poorly understood developments being implemented in schools. The general aim of this series is to take a longer term view of the changes which are occurring, to move beyond the immediate problems of implementation and to interrogate the claims and the changes in terms of broader research evidence that derives from both theoretical and empirical work. In reviewing the field in this way the intention of the series is to identify key factors and principles that should underpin the developments taking place, and provide teachers and administrators with a basis for informed decision-making that takes the educational issues seriously and goes beyond simply accommodating the latest policy imperative – difficult as even this has been in recent years!

At the same time, however, it is important to recognize that further new thinking on assessment is being severely circumscribed by present circumstances and it is for this reason that this new book by Malcolm Ross and his colleagues is so welcome. The book takes the substantive focus of assessment in the arts as an opportunity to think beyond the current verities of National Assessment and explore the role of pupil self-appraisal and self-reflection in formative assessment. It offers a vastly different perspective from that which is currently dominant, focusing on the development of self-knowledge through the processes of aesthetic understanding and aiming to explore pupils' 'capacity for making meaning in the arts'.

Ross *et al.* argue that the non-compulsory status of the arts in the National Curriculum and National Assessment programme, although threatening in some respects, also offers an opportunity for experiment, and they describe the findings of a collaborative project which set out to discover how teachers assessed in the arts, but developed into an exploration of what assessment in the arts might become. The work also carries implications for other subject areas, particularly with respect to what might be accomplished by a more reflective and interactive approach to Records of Achievement (see Christopher Pole's book in this series). Ross *et al.* develop the idea of an assessment 'conversation' between teacher and pupil, the purpose of which is not (or not only) to find out retrospectively what 'has been learned' but also to act as an educative encounter in its own right – thus treating assessment as 'the grounds not for closure but for new discoveries, new learning'.

In developing this idea Ross's team uncovered many traditional attitudes towards assessment and assumptions about the teacher–pupil role in even such an apparently flexible field as arts education. They state, 'Our teachers tended to use the conversation to confirm that the lesson had been learnt. They were not really looking to penetrate the unknown in the child's perception', and 'a new role emerges for the teacher: to equip the student with the reflective skills to monitor and assess their own work'. The research team itself then worked on developing examples of what more reflective and penetrative conversations might look like. In this respect what they report might seem to over-romanticize the pupil's capacity to respond, and certainly the research team freely admit that what they come up with presents an enormous challenge to the practicalities of everyday schooling. Yet the strength of the book is that it articulates, and presents examples of, an alternative vision of the purpose and process of assessment. Ross's work certainly cannot be thought of as something which could be easily accommodated within current practice, but it does offer a possible alternative source of thinking and experience from that which is currently so dominant. More such alternatives are needed to prevent the educational debate narrowing too far – the 'gene pool' needs to be increased if thinking in assessment is to be developed further.

Harry Torrance

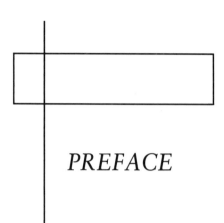

PREFACE

Curriculum practice in the arts, including assessment, tends to focus on the productive mode of the pupil's experience: making art and grading what has been made. The criteria deployed in respect of pupils' arts products are largely derived from the conventional wisdom of arts teachers – sometimes heavily dependent upon their so-called 'gut reactions' – about what constitutes a good picture, poem, musical composition, dance or drama. Recent innovations in the GCSE examination have extended this emphasis upon 'making' by demanding more practical, creative work from arts subjects such as music and English, which, in the past, have tended to adopt a more academic stance. Not that the academic study of the arts has been abandoned: students are still expected to write essays about the arts.

There is currently a powerful lobby in arts education that advocates giving more time to the study and criticism of the cultural heritage in an attempt to correct what is seen as an imbalance in the arts curriculum. There has at the same time been a move to allow for the accrediting of arts 'process', and pupils are now encouraged, even required, to document the progress of an art project from inception to completion. Assessing process and critical studies in addition to grading pupils' own art products is seen as providing a broader base for judging pupil achievement and as allowing a greater measure of objectivity in appraisals that might otherwise be considered too personal and subjective.

Largely absent from current assessment practice in the arts is any serious encouragement of the pupil's own act of self-appraisal: it is not usual for teachers to make time to sit down with their pupils to talk upon their making and help them weigh up their achievement. Nevertheless, this is our proposal. The word 'assess' is derived from the Latin *ad* + *sedere*, meaning 'to sit down together'. We are proposing that teachers and pupils should indeed sit down together in regular shared acts of assessment through talk.

The project on which this book is based aimed to give the pupils a voice, a place, in the assessment of their aesthetic activities and, at the same time, to allow the teacher's assessment to take full account of the pupils' subjective worlds – that world where their particular aesthetic projects are conceived and their unique aesthetic judgements are made. Traditionally, 'subjectivity' (of the pupil and of the teacher-assessor) has been a problem for teaching and assessment in the arts. This is because arts teachers operate largely outside their pupils' expressive acts. We, for our part, have made subjectivity central in our account of assessment in the arts. Our chosen vehicle is pupil–teacher *talk*: assessment in and through conversation.

> Because the spoken word is such a natural form of communication, building in opportunities for oral assessment is a powerful way of ensuring that pupils are given increased access to the curriculum and a greater range of opportunities to demonstrate what they know, understand and can do. Assessment through talk increases the *educational validity* of assessment by providing pupils with a way of revealing their abilities that can closely match the way talk is used outside school. If pupils are able to discuss, cross-question, present and review ideas, in contexts which are *authentic* – with audiences which are genuinely involved, and for purposes which are to do with learning, as well as with assessment – then they will be using and developing language 'for real'. In addition, they will be assessed using contexts which match pupils' experiences in the classroom. As a consequence of this,

more pupils will have the chance to reveal a wide range of ability than would be likely if assessment was solely based on written tasks.

(National Oracy Project 1991: 7)

Arts teachers have always used talk in the classroom to promote learning and reflection. They have not, in our view, exploited the potential of talk to reveal the quality of a pupil's aesthetic understanding, either in the context of instruction or of assessment – tending to rely overmuch, as the Oracy Project claims, upon written and, we would add, practical tasks. In the project reported here we have chosen to focus upon pupil–teacher talk as providing what the National Oracy Project calls 'a window on learning'.

It might be that arts teachers will decide that pupils ought to be able to talk intelligently and intelligibly about their art work and the works of other artists – in which case they may want to draw up criteria for the assessment *of* talk. Our concern, however, has been with the potential of talk as a medium for assessing knowledge, understanding and practice in the different arts subjects – with assessment *through* talk. With the National Oracy Project we believe that talk not only provides a rich and highly appropriate means of learning more about our pupils' learning; it also serves to empower the pupils, to engage and involve them directly in the assessment process. We shall go further and propose that the emphasis in the evaluation of arts practice should pass (and indeed may confidently be passed) to the pupils themselves. At the very least we would expect a 'negotiated' outcome to what has to be a collaborative undertaking in which formative appraisals – the very stuff of the teaching–learning process – provide the living ground of summative assessments.

Our proposal repositions the pupil's creative artwork in the assessment process. It becomes the subject of an ongoing conversation between pupils and teachers, the purpose of which is to prompt an expansion and deepening of the pupils' self-understanding and to give the teacher a unique opportunity to explore the pupils' capacity for reflection as part of their experience in the arts. The artwork is no longer required to serve as an exemplary, conclusive instance of the pupil's competence. Rather, it forms the basis of an illuminating encounter, yielding deep insights into the quality of the pupil's aesthetic understanding, through the medium of 'sensible' (feelingful) talk.

In Chapter 5 (Conclusion) we touch upon the practical implications of giving greater weight to the role of talk in developing and assessing aesthetic understanding – in terms of both the content and balance of the arts curriculum, and the behaviours and interrelationships of pupils and teachers. New practices demand new interpersonal structures. We are concerned to break up the monopoly rights currently exercised through assessment by the teacher upon the pupil's personal creative work – exercised as much during so-called formative as in summative assessment.

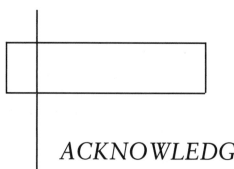

ACKNOWLEDGEMENTS

We are grateful to staff and pupils of the secondary schools working with us in our research. The project team received generous assistance from everyone, wherever we went. We hope the research outcomes will prove sufficiently stimulating to justify that support and commitment. Names of schools and of school personnel have not been given so as to protect confidentiality. It goes without saying that our greatest debt has to be to the Leverhulme Trust for their interest in our field of enquiry and support of the work.

1

CONTEXTUALIZING THE PROJECT

The arts in education

The Project was conceived and carried through in a climate of reform in education. In 1988, following years of debate about the content of the school curriculum and the effectiveness of teaching methods – a debate triggered more than ten years earlier by the then Labour Prime Minister, James Callaghan, in his famous Ruskin College speech – the Conservative Secretary of State for Education brought radically new measures before Parliament, embodied in his Education Reform Act. At the heart of the new Act was the proposal for a National Curriculum. Attainment targets and programmes of study would be laid down for some ten 'foundation subjects' and a programme of national testing drawn up to monitor children's progress at ages 7, 11, 14 and 16. These reforms were seen by their advocates as providing the only certain way of raising standards of educational performance and of providing parents and politicians with reliable information about how the education system was working. They were associated with a range of other measures designed to reduce the autonomy of local authorities, to give increased scope for policy-making and appraisal (quality control) to central government, and to introduce the principle of market economics into school management and local provision. Part of this general strategy aimed to give parents wider choice and a greater say in their children's education.

The reaction of teachers and other educational practitioners was mixed. The general principle of an entitlement curriculum that would raise standards all round was broadly welcomed. However, faced with legislation to back up imposed syllabuses and testing programmes, educationalists felt acutely threatened, and their fears were increased as new bodies were set up to oversee the implementation of the proposals and to advise the Minister, which appeared to give only restricted scope to the representation of the views of the professional. The subject-based model upon which the curriculum was to be based seemed to conflict directly with received wisdom and presaged a whole range of measures and decisions that were interpreted as turning the clock back – to practices more reminiscent of the 1950s and 1940s, some would say even earlier. Ministers were eventually to condemn the progressive practices of the 1960s and 1970s – project work in primary schools, course work in secondary schools – as questionable 'dogma', beloved of the professionals but palpably failing the children, many of whom were deemed to be emerging from the schools unable to read or compute, and lacking the technical and scientific skills the nation needed.

Having established the basic legislation, the Government proceeded to flesh it out with considerable energy. A framework for curriculum design and assessment was generated as the basis for detailed planning by subject working groups. These groups, while including teachers, were predominantly lay in membership, reflecting the Government's declared commitment to taking a practical and pragmatic view of schooling. The groups were chaired by distinguished public persons – not always academics, rarely school teachers – and always carried strong representation from employers and industry. The PE Working Party, for instance, included a professional footballer and an Olympic athlete. As the groups reported and the statutory consultation processes were entered into, it became customary to find significant sections of the different subject communities protesting – often quite strenuously – against what were seen variously as reactionary or over-prescriptive proposals. Minor adjustments were sometimes secured but the momentum of reform was not allowed to falter and the first programmes of study and testing schedules were in place for the beginning of the 1991 school year (for English, science and maths). Legislation requiring schools to publish the test and examination results and for local authorities to publish 'league tables' in which schools would be seen as competing with each other in attracting pupils followed the initial Bill.

All this could hardly have been experienced by the educational practitioner as anything other than shocking – even by those in broad sympathy with the changes and persuaded by the Government's arguments. Both the substance and the manner of the reforms were in striking contrast with school life as most serving teachers and educationalists had known it in the 1960s and 1970s. Those had been the years in which the profession – and the teacher unions in particular – had exercised undisputed influence and authority. The reforms of the early 1970s were driven by the widely held view that children should be encouraged to stay at school longer and by the need to find new ways of motivating such children to learn. This was also the time, internationally, when traditional methods were seen as restrictive and coercive, and when teachers were asked to help children become more independent, more creative and more responsible for their own learning. In 1964 a national programme of curriculum development was initiated in England and Wales by the Schools Council – a body dominated by teacher unions and eventually wound up (in 1984) on that account. A new body took over, the Schools Curriculum Development Committee – this time representing a partnership between central government and local education authorities. But this organization could not survive the agenda of Margaret Thatcher's educational advisers and was broken up in its turn with the onset of National Curriculum legislation. It was replaced by the National Curriculum Council (1988), an advisory body selected and appointed directly by the Secretary of State for Education.

What we see in this narrative is a radical shift of balance in transactions over educational policy-making. Government was no longer to hold the professional practitioner in deference. Indeed, we have seen a succession of hard-line Ministers force a radical redefinition of their professional status upon teachers. The process began, ominously, with the collapse of the teachers' last national strike in 1986 (following years of minor disruptions) and the withdrawal by Government of teachers' negotiating rights over salaries (still suspended at the time of writing). Many teachers now feel that they have lost status and public esteem, and that the National Curriculum has imposed unwelcome levels of constraint and direction upon their professional lives. In effect, while schools – and individual teachers – will have lost considerable autonomy over the curriculum, they are being given a much freer hand to manage the financing and resourcing of their operations. As already stated, local authorities have been similarly reined in, giving Ministers the possibility of exercising more direct and more immediate influence upon what happens in classrooms. The last move in a complex but single-minded strategy has been to redesign teacher training. In essence the plan is to cut back on educational theory and give schools, rather than colleges and universities, the responsibility of training the new practitioner. With the substance of children's educational experience already determined and with a repository of approved materials to draw upon, the new recruit to teaching is seen as needing practice in classroom management and induction into the new procedures for curriculum *delivery* and pupil *assessment*. A radically new professionalism has been described – to be inculcated through the mastercraftsman–apprentice model.

How have the arts fared in these turbulent times? Some would answer, 'none too well'. From the outset, the position of the arts – if we think about visual art, drama, dance, music and literature collectively – appeared problematic. Given the subject-based model informing the National Curriculum it was essential that each of the arts should be named separately, as a 'foundation subject'. In the event, only art and music were so named. Drama was to be provided for within English (on the somewhat outmoded notion that plays were a form of literature) and dance within physical education (as an aesthetic extension of gymnastics). The arts community immediately divided between those advocating 'resistance' on the basis of a subject-centred strategy and those wishing to protect and promote a more collectivist approach. An amendment to the Bill that would have substituted the words 'the Arts' for the two separate subjects music and art was narrowly defeated. Thereafter, each art subject made the best of fighting its own corner as the various Working Groups were appointed and their proposals became known. It was observed that in every case, despite serious initial misgivings over the composition of the groups appointed by Ministers, subject specialists by and large were able to support the spirit and in many cases even the letter of what was eventually proposed. The groups had clearly found much to value in what they had seen and learnt as they researched practice in schools, and had been able to translate 'good practice' into attainment targets and programmes of study that specialist secondary teachers and non-specialist primary teachers recognized and felt would be practicable.

Setbacks, some seen as serious, then occurred. As the full impact of the reforms was translated into teacher workloads and school timetables, it rapidly became clear to Ministers that modifications of the grand design would be essential if the whole system was not to break down. It came as no real surprise when music and art were singled out and made optional (rather than compulsory) at 14+. Teachers of these subjects protested vehemently at what they felt to be an unjust marginalization of their interests. Shortly afterwards dance was made optional at 11+. The notion that the arts were to be treated differently from the rest of the curriculum had been built into the provisions of the Act from the outset. There was to be no statutory system of national testing for the arts – teachers were to be responsible for pupil assessment – and no breakdown of broad attainment targets into statutory statements signalling ten levels of achievement. A strong lobby drawing teachers from across the whole range of arts subjects argued against the arts being seen as exceptional, thereby attracting low status and a soft image in comparison with the rest of the curriculum, deemed worthy and fit for hard appraisal. In the event, the National Curriculum Council advised the Secretary of State that the Art and Music Working Party proposals were too complex and impracticable, and sought to simplify directions to schools. A storm of protest by national artists, orchestral conductors, composers and ballet dancers secured a measure of adjustment, but in the final analysis there could be no getting away from the markedly different character of the legislation in respect of the arts when compared with the rest of the foundation curriculum. In the opinion of many teachers the arts lacked the authority accorded to other subjects – given their optional status at the top end of schooling and the soft arrangements judged appropriate for their monitoring and evaluation. On the other hand a view developed (the project was inclined to endorse it) that the final arrangement allowed a welcome measure of freedom to the arts, creating the essential space for experimentation and innovation while establishing for the first time a basic arts entitlement for all children during their years of formal education.

So much for the general picture. To judge where the project sits within the context of arts education itself, we need to look a little more closely at the issues that have surfaced during the period described above. If the climate for education at large could be described as turbulent, it has been no less so for teachers of the arts. The Great Education Debate initiated by Premier Callaghan in 1978 spelt danger to the arts. All the talk was of science and technology, of a 'core curriculum' that would extend only to English and maths, of the need for education to have a strong vocational emphasis. The arts community responded through the Gulbenkian Report. *The Arts in Schools*, published in 1982 and widely welcomed as a lucid and businesslike account of the role of the arts in a balanced curriculum, stressed what came to be known as the instrumental as well as the arts-specific outcomes of participation in arts programmes. The Report gave rise to a national Project of the same name, under the direction of Ken Robinson, which aimed to publicize good practice and to encourage local authorities to establish their own local networks of schools committed to excellence in the arts. At about the same time the Department of Education and Science, as part of a concerted effort to rationalize the assessment of performance in the education system, established a task group to consider assessment within the field of aesthetic development. The group's Report (1983) contained an assessment framework, which became influential over the next few years as new schemes for assessment in the arts were called for. This was a time when each of the arts subjects saw the importance of promoting itself by increasing the numbers of children entering public examinations at 16+. If the Gulbenkian Report was seen as promoting courses and administrative arrangements that linked the arts in education – not least as an effective political stratagem – there were also factions within each of the individual arts camps committed to working out separate salvations. In particular the organization claiming to represent teachers of art and design, the National Society for Education in Art and Design (a trade union in its own right), mounted a rigorous campaign of promoting its own separate interests; for a while, music, dance and drama teachers were talking actively of forming some kind of collective association, but art and design remained determinedly isolationist. The announcement of separate working parties for art and music (with none devoted specifically to dance or drama) appeared to vindicate their stance. NSEAD became closely identified with the Art Working Group and was therefore especially aggrieved when its final recommendations were tampered with by the NCC.

The hurly-burly of politically driven debate and negotiation revolved around a number of issues. Foremost, naturally, was the issue of survival: would there be life for the arts after the Education Reform Act? As we have seen, in the event it would appear that life for some of the arts, for some of the time, was assured. Ministers were to insist that schools had considerable scope, having fulfilled their obligations with respect to the National Curriculum, to provide as much arts education as they felt they wanted. It follows that schools themselves, and arts teachers within schools, would determine their own programmes in the light of their particular circumstances. We would argue that the arts could turn the freedoms they uniquely enjoy under the new system to their advantage, developing new courses and pioneering new forms of assessment. Indeed, the present project connects with this more optimistic perception. We hold strongly to the view that school heads and governors will wish not only to preserve but also to promote the arts at a time when schools need to see themselves as balanced, humane and cultured communities, concerned as much with the quality of their pupils' lives and with the promotion of civilised values as with producing a skilled and literate citizenry.

Informing the survival debate has been a deeper heart-searching about the aims of an arts education for all, its legitimate focus of study, its so-called 'knowledge-base', teaching methods and modes of assessment. A full discussion of this cluster of issues would probably take us back to Aristotle and Plato – the influence of whose analyses and arguments are still powerfully felt today. Such an excursion would be inappropriate here, as would a detailed history of the roles of the different arts in society and in education. Suffice to say that a *full* understanding of the present circumstances of arts education in the UK is impossible without recourse to a historical review. It is not for nothing that music has the longest history in education and was first studied as a science;

that art entered the curriculum as a practical subject with a specific design emphasis; that drama has, one way or another, acquired associations in the popular mind with psychotherapy and the politics of the Left. Attempts to disclose and articulate a common philosophy, a shared practice, have not dealt very successfully with these different histories. In the early 1970s Ross and Witkin sought, through a series of publications, to theorize the expressivist account of art that informed the arts curriculum, as a way of lending coherence and discipline to what arts teachers claimed they were doing, i.e. promoting children's personal development through imaginative, creative arts activities.

A recent survey suggests that this remains the overarching theory that shapes and drives the teaching of most arts practitioners in schools. However, as the present project was to discover, there remains a serious discontinuity between that theory (those declared aims) and teaching and learning practices in schools. We shall be suggesting that part of the problem lies in the tension arts teachers often feel between the way they would like to work and relate to their students and what the institution (the school, the system) expects and permits. Another important factor contributing to teacher stress and confusion is the issue of legitimate knowledge. In the past few years this debate has focused upon ideas of tradition, the canon, the teaching of what is called visual or aural 'literacy' – i.e. upon training in the understanding and interpretation of art and music as special, culturally specific languages or symbolic codes. These topics have been seen as affording a more defensible content for arts subjects in the curriculum than more nebulous ideas about expression and personal development. It is precisely this strongly *rational* stance that has been endorsed by the different working parties with the perhaps initially surprising outcome that the majority of arts teachers find themselves, at the end of what seemed a potentially disastrous process, pretty comfortable with the perceptions and pronouncements of the Government. Differences are a matter of detail and emphasis – the Minister was besieged principally by fine artists and classical musicians, not by rap artists, reggae dancers or punk bands or indeed anyone from the theatre at all. These, one senses, are artists for whom the arts in schools may mean very little. And that is entirely understandable since what is being officially proposed for the arts in the National Curriculum is essentially the time-honoured formula of school art, otherwise known as safe art, a diluted (some have said an enviscerated) experience of the Western classical, high art tradition.

Arts teachers by and large would want to maintain that knowledge in the arts – a kind of practical know-how that facilitates acts of authentic expression and communication – counts more than knowledge *about* the arts; that you tell good work from poor work in the arts through some kind of gut reaction, intuitively. As with actual teaching itself, in assessment arts teachers often feel they know more than they can say.

The assessment context

Arts education encourages individual creative responses and needs an appropriate assessment methodology that genuinely reflects the expressive and creative dimensions of art. However, assessing what has been learnt by the child in this artistic experiencing has been problematic for teachers within the traditional assessment mode that predominates in UK schools.

Within objectivity-focused assessment, arts teachers have developed skills and expertise in assessing the *outcome* of the process of realizing feeling in form, the manifestation of the individual subjective sense of experiencing aesthetically. The product or artefact is viewed from a number of perspectives and informed judgements are made by 'experts' on the quality of the artwork. The teachers also assess those aspects of the process that they feel able to access through observation of the pupils at work. They follow criteria that require them to grade the way the pupils perform the task, how they interact with the artistic medium, how they work with others (when appropriate) and so on. What is left implicit and inaccessible to objective scrutiny and/or observation within this mode of assessing is the subjective intention and inner emotional (affective) and intellectual (cognitive) struggle that makes up the creative process.

Teachers recognize the limitations of an assessment model that appears to overvalue the outcome of the expressive act and observed practice but undervalue the aesthetic qualities, the personal expressive sensibilities that inspire the pupils to artistic creativity. This aspect of the process is considered irrelevant in an assessment mode that concentrates primarily on fulfilling the purpose for which it is designed: grading the pupils in a rank order of merit based on socially constructed standards of what constitutes good to poor achievement, on a scale of measurement against common criteria (criterion-referenced assessment) or against each other (norm-referenced assessment), or a mixture of both.

It was upon this sense of shared unease between arts teachers and researchers over the assessment of creative work in schools that the Exeter-based Leverhulme Project elected to focus. It was felt by the participants in the project that a form of assessment that takes due account of the personal, expressive, as well as collective, instructional objectives of arts curricula was largely absent from most contemporary practice. This problem seriously threatens to undermine the educational status of arts education within the National Curriculum, where the emphasis on assessing and reporting achievement for accountability purposes has become a predominant issue.

The aesthetic qualities and understandings that the pupils bring to their work are valued by arts teachers as an important dimension of art experience. Teachers claim to be developing these qualities. The central research questions in our project were organized around the creative challenge of devising a valid and comprehensive assessment strategy that would yield qualitative information about and do full justice to the pupils' artistic achievements. We focused on this issue in the belief that such information would help teachers to support pupils in further developing their aesthetic understanding, which in turn would enhance the pupils' creative and expressive endeavours.

Assessment research and innovative practice in the UK and other countries provided us with a framework to orientate our inquiry and investigation. Traditionally assessment has been synonymous with examinations, conceived as a competitive device designed to select out the more academically able from the less able pupils. As Roach succinctly puts it: 'Public examinations were the great discovery of the nineteenth-century Englishman. Almost unknown at the beginning of the century, they rapidly became a major tool of social policy' (Roach 1971: 3). The present 16+ examination system (the General Certificate of Secondary Education) exemplifies the way that the twin notions of selection and competition have driven the assessment system to operate on two levels. At the level of the individual, the pupils' grades in the examinations determine the kind of education and/or training they will have access to from 16 to 19, where there is competition for finite resources. At the institutional level, these notions of selection and competition are reinforced by the structure of the examination, which, introduced nationally, prescribed criteria in all the major subjects of the curriculum. The existence of common criteria has given the politicians a basis for establishing the idea that schools' educational achievements could be reasonably judged through comparing the GCSE results of one school with another. These two notions of selection and competition have been transposed into the new arrangements for National Curriculum assessment. The GCSE has become the final assessment point in a centrally imposed assessment scheme that has external, standardized assessments for all children at ages 7, 11 and 14 as well as 16.

Over the past seven years, since the introduction of the GCSE, political emphasis in the educational arena has increasingly concentrated on promoting this accountability aspect of assessment. This is clearly demonstrated by the developments in the debate between educationalists and politicians with regard to the design of the national assessments at key ages 7 and 14. The Secretary of State, through the DES, set up a group of educational experts to advise on assessment and testing within the National Curriculum. The recommendations from the report of this group, the Task Group on Assessment and Testing (TGAT), were closely followed by the test constructors of the pilot Standard Assessment Tasks (SATs). However, the Secretary of State for Education under the powers granted him by the Education Reform Act (1988) decided to reformulate and simplify substantially the pilot SATs after the first round of trials, which indicated severe levels of overload among the participating schools. The Secretary of State's action to limit SATs to mainly pencil and paper tests has reduced the breadth and variety of educational achievements open to standardized national assessment.

The political intrusion into educational practice with stress on the accountability dimension of assessment has been addressed by educational researchers (Broadfoot *et al.* 1990). Torrance (1989) also points this out in reviewing developments in the field of assessment over the past ten or fifteen years. He cites arguments by assessment analysts who perceive a shift away from the traditional quantification model of assessment to a broader conceptualization owing to the traditional form's allegedly exerting 'an unduly restricting influence on the curriculum and on the process of teaching' (Torrance 1989: 184).

This 'restricting influence', if given free rein, could become a powerful force in controlling and ordering curriculum practices of teachers, raising issues about the relationship of assessment to learning and pupil motivation. The issue has been on the agenda of concerns for assessment researchers and analysts for a number of years. Concerns have also been expressed about the negative effects failure in examinations has on low-achieving pupils. Furthermore, the psychological effects that school failure is seen to have on the future life chances of pupils is perceived to be detrimental when the child leaves the school system with no record of his or her abilities or positive achievements (Hargreaves 1982; Broadfoot 1979, 1984).

These psychological arguments have had a marked influence on assessment practices. The result has been a shift from selection as the prime function of assessment to a more inclusive definition, encompassing the notion that educational assessment should provide a broader range of information about pupils' accomplishments. This, in turn, leads to developing assessment strategies that offer insights into the learning process in order both to reveal achievements already gained and to improve learning strategies. (Tyler 1986; Wood 1987; Frederikson and Collins 1989; Paris *et al.* 1991).

This wider conceptualization of assessment is recognizable in the definition of assessment offered by Rowntree:

> One person in some kind of interaction, direct or indirect with another, is conscious of obtaining and interpreting information about the knowledge and understanding, or abilities and attitudes of that other person.
>
> (Rowntree 1977: 4)

Rowntree perceives the art of assessing as a human encounter that involves information gathering and the interpretation of that information. One human being is placing value on the attitudes, acts, activities and achievements of another human being: making qualitative judgements about what that person knows, understands and can do. As a means of gathering and evaluating information – the possibility of assessment having a purpose in education other than selection – the parameters of assessment have been expanded. These purposes can broadly be categorized as either formative or summative. An example of a formative purpose would be to support learning through information being gathered to enable teachers to identify strengths and weaknesses in pupils' skills and knowledge, and then to feed that information back to the pupils themselves while they work. The sharing of this information between pupil and teacher could, in Vygotsky's (1972) terms, encourage the move from the current level of the pupil's development to the potential level of development – 'the zone of next development'. Summative assessment – when information is gathered through the pupil and the teacher working on the gathering process together – describes, in some contextual detail, the actual achievements of the pupil. Descriptive statements, in the form of a profile, could be written to 'sum up' the pupil's achievements.

These interactive, collaborative modes of assessment are now part of many teachers' repertoire of assessment skills deployed as part of classroom practice. These skills have become more centrally, over the past decade, an important dimension of the teacher's role as a professional educator. As Peter Mitchell states:

> In essence pedagogical knowledge is concerned with planning, assessing and evaluating students' learning. It involves interpreting aims into practice and having ways of assessing students' achievements which grow out of the purposes behind the classroom experiences.
>
> (Mitchell 1989: 8)

Teacher assessment within the National Curriculum programme is intended to continue concurrently with the proposed 'external' SATs, and need not be reduced to a narrow conception of assessment that mirrors the externally constructed assessments. It is possible to conceive of teacher assessments as offering the prospect of developing new modes of assessing that reflect the acceptance of the teacher as a professional educator.

As the Schools Examination and Assessment Council's broadsheet (1991) on Teacher Assessment at Key Stage 3 states:

> Teacher assessment is an integral part of teaching and learning in the classroom. Teachers discuss with pupils, guide their work, ask and answer questions, observe, encourage,

challenge, help and focus. In addition they mark and review written work and other outcomes. Through these activities they are continually finding out about their pupils' capabilities and achievements. This knowledge then informs plans for future work. It is this continuous process that comprises teacher assessment.

(SEAC 1991)

The project's approach to assessment has been influenced by two fundamental beliefs: first, recognition of the purpose of assessment as informing and improving learning; second, placing both the teacher and the pupil at the heart of the process.

Sally Brown (1990) discusses this new approach to assessment in the following way:

Change can be unsettling, sometimes overwhelming, but it can also be motivating and bring about real progress. In the field of assessment, a great deal of talk over the last decade has been about change and substantial attempts have been made to introduce new practices. Different practices usually reflect different ideological commitments, and one of the most salient features of the movement has been the recognition that assessment, as part of education, must be about promoting learning and opportunities, rather than sorting people into social roles for society.

(Brown 1990: 5)

She articulates four particular themes which draw out certain principles that are supportive of our approach to the problem of assessment.

The first theme is the broader conceptualization of assessment. Assessment is no longer to be equated simply with testing and, through testing, selection. Assessment is to be seen to fulfil multiple purposes. The TGAT (1988) Report, set up to devise the structure for National Curriculum assessment, attempts to interrelate within a single system these multiple purposes. Para. 23 states that 'assessment (including tests) shall be capable of serving several purposes: formative, diagnostic, summative, and evaluative.' In this system, classroom and external assessment are meshed together (Macintosh 1988), with formative and summative assessment seen as complementary, as described in Paras 26 and 27 of the Report:

We judge therefore that an assessment system designed for formative assessment can meet all the needs of national assessment at ages before 16.

(Para. 23)

We recommend that the basis of the national assessment system be essentially formative. At age 16, however, it should incorporate assessment with summative functions.

(Para. 27)

The TGAT group's perceptions of the different approaches to assessing, i.e. the making of qualitative judgements by teachers as a necessary counterbalance to quantifiable, externally set objective tests is clearly expressed in the 'purposes and principles' section of the Report. Para. 42 states:

In a narrower sense, the term 'assessment' is used to refer to an individual component of the total assessment process or to a particular method of assessment. Hence, it encompasses all procedures used to make an estimate or appraisal of an individual's achievement. Which of the many methods of assessment may be appropriate in particular circumstances will depend on the purpose of the assessment.

In the aesthetic area, the process of developing an understanding and awareness of personal meaning is paramount. In the project's view the principle of personal development outweighs all other principles and purposes of assessment in the context of aesthetic education.

The second of Brown's innovative themes is the recognition that it is now possible, through this broader conceptualization of assessment, to assess a wide range of qualities. Certain qualities, e.g. critical thinking, self-knowledge, invention, formulating new questions or making inferences, are not susceptible to being assessed through highly structured, standardized assessment tasks that provide information on the acquisition and application of knowledge. Assessment strategies that focus on the product of pupils' thinking rarely offer qualitative insights into the thinking process.

This issue of acquiring assessment skills in getting to know how well students learn has been an important research question for American assessment agencies in recent years (Nuttall 1991; and illustrated through interviews in *Educational Researcher* in 1991).

More specific, and of particular interest to us, are the findings of the American research into assessment in the arts funded by the Rockefeller Foundation in 1985 to develop 'powerful versions' of qualitative modes of assessment:

> The lack of powerful qualitative information about student learning, thoughtful ways of using that information, and training for educators in this kind of assessment is a major gap in the way American educators go about indexing and studying student learning.
>
> (Wolf 1988)

This study found ways of tapping into the essential qualities of art education – individuality and invention – by focusing on assessment modes that made visible the individual's ability to formulate novel problems, engage in a number of thinking processes and reflect on the quality of his or her own work. The 'making visible' was achieved by teachers refining their assessment skills through 'reading' their students' 'biographies' of progress as demonstrated in the students' portfolios and engaging in reflective interviews with the students, which gave an opportunity for teachers and students together to stand back and think about the artwork the student had produced.

In our assessment we are concerned with the principle of *making visible* qualities that celebrate individual uniqueness, qualities that cannot be either profitably or easily registered as comparative and standardized, measurable units.

The third of Brown's themes relates to the incorporation of descriptive statements into the educational assessment system alongside the giving of marks and grades. We endorse the principle of pupils receiving summary documents that describe actual achievements when it relates directly with Brown's fourth theme, the devolution of responsibility for assessment to agencies outside the examination boards, because we perceive that the process of generating the descriptive statements opens up assessment strategies to pupil participation in and contribution to his or her own assessment. The two principles, articulation of achievement and self-assessment, are key factors in an assessment strategy that is designed to illuminate aesthetic processes.

In summary, these four key principles correspond closely with the project's approach to devising a qualitative assessment strategy that generates information about the pupils' understanding in the aesthetic domain of arts education: personal development, the stressing of individual uniqueness, the articulation and appraisal of creative achievements, the 'assessed' persons responsible for assessing themselves.

In the initial phase of the project, which entailed discussions with arts teachers in order to focus on an appropriate line of inquiry from their point of view, the teachers told us that they were formatively assessing their pupils' creative and aesthetic responses implicitly during normal classroom interactions. Teachers suggested to us that when they talked to pupils about their creative work it gave both the pupils and themselves the chance to reflect on and think about the qualities of the ongoing work. These conversations influenced the ongoing cumulative judgements the teachers were making regarding the creative and aesthetic development of their pupils. They were still relying, however, in the main on unexamined and implicit criteria.

We reasoned that a positive task for the project would be to attempt to exploit and expand the kind of formative assessment practice we had observed by devising an assessment strategy that gave greater scope for reflection and made more deliberate use of pupil–teacher talk. Talk, especially when it is exploratory (Barnes 1976) is eminently suitable as a way of engaging with one another's feelings, ideas, perceptions and values. Talk is used in the form of conversations for such purposes every day. Barnes argues, with reference to Sapir (1949), Vygotsky (1972) and Bruner (1966), that speech enables us to control thought: 'Through language we both *receive* a meaningful world from others, and at the same time *make meanings* by interpreting that world to our own ends' (Barnes 1976: 101).

Schön's (1983) definition of the 'reflective practitioner' exemplifies our concept of the teacher as a professional educator. In particular, his notion of the 'reflective conversation' affirms the strategy we uncovered for ourselves in wrestling with the specific problems we encountered as we began to study assessment practices in the project schools. Schön suggests that the notion of the reflective practitioner offers an alternative way forward for professionals who do not see their future in increasing bureaucratization (i.e. as sophisticated technicians). Arts education traditionally conforms to Schön's model of 'technical rationality'. A somewhat bizarre collusion between the arts education establishment and the architects of the National Curriculum threatens to convert arts teachers – as the legislation is specifically designed to do – into a new breed of professionals no longer resting their case upon their exclusive expertise but operating as sophisticated technicians on the floor of a highly automated industrial plant. Art practice, on the other hand, is a paradigm of Schön's alternative model – what he calls 'reflective conversation with the situation'. Arts teachers need to consider which road they now wish to follow. Our own view is that they might perhaps take the lead in pioneering radical teaching practices that would revitalize the education system, providing an alternative to the new orthodoxy of the Right, and holding fast to arts practice that explores and celebrates children's lives through participation in *authentic arts experiences*.

2

THE PROJECT'S HISTORY

Research methods

The research methods employed in this project were qualitative: we considered it important to come to an understanding of the reality of the situation in the schools at the level of the interactions that were taking place between teachers and pupils in the learning and assessing process. It was a 'multi-site' qualitative study in the sense that we visited a number of different research sites, investigating the same research problem and using similar data collection and analysis procedures in each setting.

The research methods chiefly consisted of non-participant observation of classroom practice and interviewing of teachers and pupils. We collected the data by means of audio and video recordings as well as written notes. At various stages of the project we fed back our findings to the participants by holding one-day conferences at strategic times between different project phases. This allowed us to incorporate their responses into our research as it developed.

The project had four phases, with each phase developing out of the analysis of the data gathered in the preceding phase. This was a crucial part of our research strategy, enabling us to respond to the findings of each stage and to adjust the direction of the project to address predominant issues that emerged through the empirical evidence. After the final phase, case studies on each site were written up. These analytically descriptive case studies based upon the written, oral and videotaped material informed the final analysis.

In this chapter the story of each phase is told, indicating the dynamic–responsive nature of the project's approach.

Phase 1

In phase 1 of the research, following the appointment of the project's two research assistants early in January 1990 and the selection of the pilot schools, teachers agreeing to be part of the project were visited, interviewed and observed teaching. The fundamental research question they were asked was, what they considered to be the central concerns of their own particular arts subjects. In reply, most teachers referred especially to the expressive and creative opportunities offered to pupils in the arts. This response matched data collected from a larger sample of Cornish schools studied immediately prior to the inception of the present project (see Ross 1991).

When they were asked about assessing how pupils dealt with these opportunities, however, teachers stated that they found the expressive/creative areas elusive, difficult to define and inade-quately addressed by existing assessment procedures, which con-centrated upon easily quantifiable and observable processes and products. In their assessments of their pupils' expressive work teachers seemed to have to rely on what they called variously 'gut feeling', 'intuition' and 'experience'. The expressive dimension was recognized in formal assessment only by means of these 'gut reactions' – often amounting only to somewhat blunt expressions of the teacher's own aesthetic preferences. Many teachers were painfully aware of a conflict of role – on the one hand as represen-tatives (somehow) of the school as a social and cultural institution and so as custodians of public standards of behaviour and achieve-ment, and on the other as committed to nurturing and cherishing children, both in their own right and in terms of their personal, expressive statements.

No matter how 'democratic' the teacher is in interacting with children in the organization of classroom life, the teacher remains the leader, the pupils followers, be they enthusiastic or reluctant. Schools control pupils, and the normal teacher–pupil relationship is similarly subject to institutionalized controls. School life, fundamentally, has not changed significantly since 1932 when W. Waller wrote his classic text, *The Sociology of Teaching*, in which he states:

> Teacher and pupil confront each other in the school with an original conflict of ideas and however much that conflict may be reduced in amount, or however, much it may be hidden, it remains. The teacher represents the adult group, ever the enemy of the spontaneous life of groups of children. The teacher represents the formal curriculum, and his interest is in imposing that curriculum upon the children in the form of tasks. . . . Pupils are the material in which teachers are supposed to produce results. Pupils are human beings striving to realize themselves in their own spontaneous way, striving to produce their own results in their own way.
>
> (Waller 1932: 195–6)

The arts teachers in the project were conscious of these conflicts of interest between teachers and pupils and the amount of control and influence they had over the creative process of their pupils. One art teacher in interview articulated the general concern of many teachers in this way:

> It's quite hard keeping a balance between some sort of organizational strictness but then having everybody free and having the time and space or whatever to do what they want to do. It's quite hard keeping that balance, because, you know, if you come down really strict – I mean, I've seen it before – the kids are frightened to say, 'Actually can I do it like this, with the stripes down that way?' If you're quite fierce then they're frightened to do that. They think they're going to get a roasting because they've done it the other way up or something. I mean, that's hardly conducive to making their own decisions. But that is a very tricky thing to actually implement in the school, in these surroundings, because as soon as they think 'freedom' it can go sadly wrong very quickly. So there is definitely a conflict and you are trying to achieve something

that isn't about control or order but is about something completely different. That's difficult to achieve within the school set-up.

(Art teacher in interview, phase 1)

The arts teachers in the project behaved pedagogically in a way that strove to minimize these conflicts in an attempt to find a balance between a necessary degree of control and allowing the pupils freedom to express themselves. Generally speaking, in the arts lessons observed by the research team, the teachers encouraged pupils to use their imagination and their own ideas in the act of producing/making paintings, sculptures, musical compositions, plays, poems, etc. An environment was provided for the pupils where they had access to the materials of art making, music making and play making. The teachers provided the stimuli, the initial ideas and structures and the technical know-how and generally gave the pupils the space to get on with the task. Sometimes the task was prescribed and sometimes the pupils were given more freedom to explore their own ideas – individually (in art) or in groups (in music and drama). In many of the schools visited, the arts teachers had created a climate in the arts rooms that had a significantly different 'feel' from other classrooms in the school: e.g. black out and atmospheric lighting in the drama room; the intimate and private sense of being in an art studio; the acoustic space conducive to singing and playing together in soundproof music rooms and recording studios. The arts teachers valued their specialist spaces as centres of artistic activity where pupils could 'key into' expectations different from those associated with other subjects, where the relationship between the teachers and their pupils was often less relaxed and pupils were not so free to move around during the lesson.

Working in the predominantly affective domain, arts teachers had a more open teaching style that manifested itself in the way they communicated with their pupils. Douglas Barnes, in his book *From Communication to Curriculum* (1976), addresses the issue of pupil–teacher power relations by looking at the different forms of talk promoted and acceptable in the learning context. He identifies two uses of oral language in the classroom:

1 Talk as a means of control where the learner is in 'a passive role as the recipient of socialization' (p. 31). Here is the conflict

between control and freedom that our art teacher was referring to (pp. 21–2), i.e. the teacher has control over communication in the classroom and the pupils have clear expectations of their role as 'receivers' and the role of their teacher as the transmitter.

2 Talk as a means of learning, where the learner is actively making meaning. Through talk, the learner is able to reflect on thought processes, 'Language allows one to consider not only what one knows but how one knows it' (p. 98). Barnes argues that the pupils' ability to make meaning actively, to construct new knowledge, is greatly determined by the teacher's implicit view of what counts as or is seen as knowledge. The teacher's social control relates to his or her control of knowledge.

> Language performs two functions simultaneously: it carries the message that you are wanting to communicate and at the same time it conveys information about who you think you are, who you think you are talking to, what you believe the situation to be and so on. Whenever you talk, your speech both carries the conscious message and – usually unconsciously – negotiates the social relationships which you are taking part in.
>
> (Barnes 1976: 116)

It was to *talk* that we would eventually turn as our preferred medium for interrogating and assessing the pupil's aesthetic understanding. What arts teachers think constitutes knowledge seems to oscillate between (a) seeing knowledge as the property of the teacher as art expert proficient in practical skills, arts vocabulary and the making of aesthetic judgements, and the pupil meeting the pre-ordained criteria of good practice in each of the different arts disciplines; and (b) seeing knowledge as the pupil's interpretation of her own experience in the pursuit of personal meaning. For most teachers in the project, (a) clearly dominated over (b), and this created particular problems for us. However, very few of our teachers were unaffected by the rival claims of the two forms of knowledge. They provided many examples of their dual role as transmitters of the culture in the arts disciplines and providers of an environment to support individual exploration and the making of personal statements. One drama teacher, for example, claimed that 'my role is to provide the pupils with the techniques and the

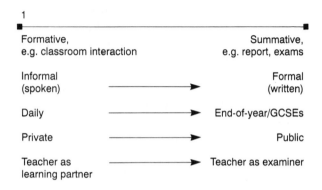

Figure 1 Formative and summative assessments compared.

vocabulary of drama to improve their skills. They can only be creative after they have managed to acquire the skills and techniques, to know the different forms that drama can take, that is what I teach them.' Another drama teacher, also concerned with skills, saw skills and expressiveness as interdependent:

> Drama lessons need to have a structure. The teacher needs to know what skills she or he is trying to develop. Skills are important in order that the pupil can express or create effectively. Teaching is about providing structure and being flexible. You have a structure, you know what you want, you think through what you want from the youngsters, what you hope the youngster will get out of it. And then you go in and if you are not getting what you want out of it then you've got to change it quickly or otherwise the youngsters lose interest and a drama lesson can be a total waste of time.

When it came to the area of assessment the teachers' views of their role could be plotted on a continuum ranging from strictly formative to strictly summative assessment. (Figure 1). The pairs of words listed below the formative and summative ends of the continuum in Figure 1 provided the teachers' definition of each polarity. The formative end is about pupil–teacher interaction within the classroom that is so integrated with teaching as to become practically indistinguishable from it. The strictly formalized summative side of assessment is comprised of end-of-year reports,

GCSE marking and exam results. In between the two polarities, most of the teachers would probably place forms of written assessment to which the students themselves contribute. Most teachers think highly of these forms of assessment, and the more highly they rate them, the nearer, probably, they would place them to the formative end. Was this because they were concerned for assessment to be beneficial to the student and, in some sense therefore, part of the learning process in which student involvement plays a crucial part? One teacher said:

> From the start you're posing questions to them and asking them to look at what they're doing, and think about what they're doing and that's what I think assessment is all about, rather than saying '4 out of 10' or '3 out of 10' in the way that you might do in other subjects. For me that is the important bit. The youngsters being able to assess what they're doing and being able to talk about what they're doing and why they're doing it.

The quotation illustrates two entirely different ways of using the word 'assessment', representing both the formative and summative ends of the continuum. The majority of teachers agree about the importance of the formative end of the continuum and that children need feedback in order to progress. Where they differ is on the degree to which this could or should be formalized. There was an inclination to consider formal assessment as summative and informal as formative and therefore they were finding it difficult to see how the involvement of pupils in the assessment process and the nature of the pupils' expressiveness could be made more explicit and identifiable rather than remaining implicit within the teaching and learning process itself.

> It is important not only that the pupils know what they're good at, but that the teacher knows this too – that is the essence of teaching.
>
> You are looking for sincerity, you are looking for commitment, you are looking for imagination and those are very, very difficult things to quantify.
>
> I feel you need to have a kind of assessment procedure which gives the opportunity for the teacher to talk directly with the individual about their strengths and weaknesses.

Yes, I open up new ways, to send in new directions, to pull back. But that's not putting a mark on it, is it?

The purpose of the project began to take shape around the idea of redressing the balance between the observable/quantifiable and the tacit/unquantifiable in assessment in order to seek ways in which the personal experience of pupils could properly be identified and valued. We decided to work alongside the teachers in developing an assessment strategy that more closely resembled, reflected and could be integrated with the facilitative role they adopted when teaching.

Phase 2

In phase 2 of the research (April to July 1990), following a one-day evaluation conference with the pilot teachers, it was decided to explore 'talk' as a medium of assessment. In particular we began to develop the idea of the 'assessment conversation', attracted particularly by the sense of mutuality, of openness and of flexibility associated with this form of verbal social interaction.

Conversation has a certain spontaneity and freedom that we felt exactly suited the delicate task of probing and appraising the quality of a pupil's expressive and creative processes. Furthermore, we wished to see if it were possible to reduce the judgemental element in assessment here, so that the student could feel confident enough in the relationship with her teacher to explore all aspects of her work – the weaknesses as well as the strengths – and reach her own verdict. Good conversations are often both free-ranging and inconclusive – features we were to refine somewhat in the light of experience. On our return to the schools we gave the teachers the following instructions:

We should like you to conduct a conversation with one of your pupils that focuses on her/his arts work (music or dance or drama or art or writing) in progress. It could be work that is currently going on or work that has been finished but that will relate to later work not yet started. The purpose of the conversation is to discuss with the student their understanding of the process which is ongoing. This is to encourage the pupil to self-assess in a formative way that will give her/him the confidence to continue to develop her/his arts work. The conversation should, therefore, be task-oriented, i.e. specific to a particular piece of work. Wherever possible the work under discussion should be present.

At this stage we were clear that we wanted the conversation to be 'real' rather than academic; that we were hoping for personal responses from the pupil rather than empty 'art-crit' speak; that we saw the conversation as tied into the learning/formative mode; that we wanted it to have a specific focus on a particular piece of work rather than, for instance, to be a general chat about art.

All conversations were recorded on video and audio tape so that they could be subsequently analysed by us and, where appropriate, discussed with the participants. This gave rise to a number of technical and personal problems. We had to master the equipment and learn to cope with difficult filming conditions; some of the teachers and pupils felt that being filmed would be a trying ordeal. There was some concern as well that the presence of camera and camerawoman would unduly inhibit the participants. All these problems were overcome satisfactorily and no one refused to be filmed. There remained the inevitable element of artificiality conse-quent upon the recording situation. However, making allowances did not prove either inherently difficult in itself or damaging to our hopes that we would be able to appraise the practical value of the construct: the assessment conversation. In the event we were disappointed to find that in many of the conversations the pupil's expressive experience was not addressed at all, and in others it was marginalized by other issues.

Here are two fairly typical conversations from phase 2. They were both recorded 'on the hoof' – i.e. here are a music teacher and then an art teacher, going about the business of formative assessment as an aspect of their day-to-day classroom teaching. Both teachers have their attention focused upon their pupils' productivity, and are concerned to get them thinking more clearly about what they might do next. These conversations should ring true for many arts teachers. It has been our experience that when introduced to our notion of assessment through talk, teachers have often said, 'Well, that's what we are doing all the time anyway.' We hope to make clear in later sections of this book our reservations about this assertion, and to establish a claim not just for talk that addresses (and values) the pupil's aesthetic experience more directly, but for more time and space for the reflective and contemplative in arts education generally – i.e. for activity that does not achieve its object in the realization (production) of an aesthetic artefact.

[Pupils play their musical piece.]

T: OK. Now do you know what you've done with that? How many times have you played each of those ideas?

P_1: About four bars.   5

T: Yes, each one's been repeated twice – well, y'know, played and then repeated. So that has its shape. So how could you perhaps start altering that?

P_1: Repeat it more times or don't repeat it . . .

T: No, you need something different, don't you?   10

Ps: Uhm.

P_2 to P_1: What we need is something totally different.

T: Well, what about trying to alter the bass first of all? Is there anything else you could do with the bass?

P_2: We could bring it down lower. Instead of going up   15 we could go down.

[Ps tinkle on piano.]

T: Try going down the scale. [Demonstrates this by singing.]

[Ps play this on the piano.]   20

P_2: Something like this?

T: Or you could play chords. Try playing chords.

[Ps play.]

T: Oh, no, you've got to have a minor chord, haven't you?

[Ps play.]   25

T: Think of your key.

[Ps play.]

T: Repeat each one. [Demonstrates this by singing.] The only trouble is that it's still very similar to what you had before, isn't it really?   30

[Ps continue to play. *T* continues to instruct and coax.]

T: How similar is that to the bass – the chords?

P_2: Same notes.

[*Ps* discuss and demonstrate this.]

T: Well, could you play something . . . Well, how about   35
[comes round to piano] . . . Where do you start?

[*Ps* demonstrate.]

T: What key are you in?

P_1: C.

T: C what?   40

P_2: C minor.

T: C minor, that's right. So [plays piano] . . . try staying on
the same note for a bit.

[*Ps* play.]

T: That's good. You see, you've got a different section   45
coming now.

P_1: It's like the 12 bar blues.

T: Well, yes, of course it is. That's fine. See if you can
work that in but then you have to get it so that it fits in
with what you've done before. So work on that section   50
now using a sort of a 12 bar blues format.

This is formative assessment in the teaching process. The teacher
is examining the artwork in an ongoing, formative, musical
encounter with the pupils: i.e the makers. Her role is dominant: she
knows the answers or, at the very least, she clearly has certain
specific musical 'moves' in mind which she wishes to elicit or coax
from – but may eventually have to supply to – her pupils. T: 'You
need something different' (10). P_2 to P_1: 'We need something
totally different' (12). Teacher supplies a point of departure ('What
about trying to alter the bass?' (13)) and pupils respond by 'going
down' instead of 'going up' (15–16). Teacher continues to lead by
supplying examples (she sings) and they imitate. She makes another
practical suggestion – 'you could play chords' (22) – and then
pushes on more assertively towards, presumably, her own solution:
'Oh, no, you've got to have a minor chord' (24). 'Think of your key'
(26). 'Repeat each one' (28). Eventually, apparently running out
of ideas (or time), she takes over at the piano to provide specific
material for them to adopt or adapt. 'Try staying on the same note
for a bit' (42–43). Somehow they arrive at 'a different section' (45),
'like the 12 bar blues' (47). The teacher is satisfied that the
'something different' has been arrived at and allows the pupils to

'work on that section . . . using a sort of a 12 bar blues format' (50–51). A technical solution has been sought and found for what was perceived essentially as a technical problem – by the teacher. She does not probe their sense of the meaning of their composition or their satisfaction with the changes she has helped to bring about in the piece; she seems impatient to move the piece along even at the price of wresting control and ownership from the pupils. (Does she conceive of such ownership; do they?) It is clear that they have certain technical 'handling' and 'knowledge' skills that allow them to 'produce' musical objects within particular specifications – but what felt or personal meaning, significance or status these might have for the pupils is hard to judge.

The next example shows a visual art teacher using his experience and skills to instruct a pupil in developing her style of drawing.

[Pupil is sitting in front of a large, dried-flower arrangement, drawing with a pencil on white cartridge paper.]

T: And what are you actually trying to do?

P: I've got the flowers and . . .

T: So you're not actually trying to . . .? 5

P: [interrupting] Draw the actual arrangement? No.

T: No. So you're just going to use it as a sort of starting point?

P: Uhuh.

T: You said to me just now . . . 10

P: [interrupting] To draw flowers, colourful flowers.

T: Yeah, you said to me 'I want some dry flowers with colour in,' didn't you?

P: Yeah, and I'm doing a black and white one [drawing] and then developing it into colour. 15

T: [Laughs.] Would it not be better to work straight in colour?

P: No. Most of the work I do at home is in colour but I always start it in black and white and then do it in colour. 20

T: You see, I can see you working there in nice thick paint, straight on . . .

P: On black paper?

T: Yeah, using the lovely sort of quality of texture and things like that. You could produce some beautiful 25

textures. You could have real fun with that. And
you'd get much more sort of a feeling of the sort of
textural quality and the way it sort of . . . I mean, look
at this here [a cluster of small white flowers in the
arrangement] and the way it sort of goes !!!!!! [*T* emits   30
explosive gun sounds with accompanying hand
gestures.]

P: It's like someone's shooting a gun.

T: It is, isn't it? It's arrested. It's almost as if it had been
shot at. [*T* makes squawking 'aargh' sound as if he'd   35
been shot in the chest. His hand is jerked violently
upwards and freezes.] And it's been stopped, y'know,
hasn't it? [*T* makes 'aargh' noise again –
like vomiting.] And this bit here [points to
yellow dandelion-like flower], you've got that lovely   40
sort of circle bit there and then it goes !!!!!!!! [*T* makes
spattering noises and, with his hand, gestures the
movement of the petals coming out from the centre.]

P: And then it's got, like, a dot in the middle of the circle.

T: Yeah, and that's . . . in a way, if you describe that . . . if   45
that process is going through your mind as you're
doing it, you're just going to do it like that. You're just
going to go !!!!!!! [Mimes actions and makes the
appropriate noises.] and then it's done. And you'll get
just as nice a spontaneous feeling as you would if   50
you were just trying to do that sort of super-accurately.

P: Everything messy looks a lot better, doesn't it?

T: Not necessarily.

P: But if you do something like that you like to do it, like,
all thick paint to make it look as if it's more realistic.   55

T: Yes, but that's the realism [points to dried flower] – that
actual flower – isn't it? And that ultimately is where the
realism is. So if you really want realism, you pick a flower.
What you're doing is . . . You're what? You're doing a . . . ?

P: Well . . .   60

T: You're just doing this as an interpretation, like you
said at the beginning. But now you're turning
yourself around and you're saying, 'I'm not doing an
interpretation, I'm trying to be realistic.'

P: Yeah.   65

> *T*: Well, you're not. You're always doing an interpretation.
> OK? So what I'd like you to do, I'd like you to get one
> of those black drawing boards, I'd like you to put it on
> there, I'll get you some black paper and I'd like you
> to go straight ahead, get straight on with it.   70

Here, in another instructional encounter, the teacher uses transactional and expressive language to saturate the pupil in an exchange geared to getting the pupil going. The teacher's agenda would appear to be to challenge and change the pupil's preferred way of working, no matter what. The urgency in the teacher's approach is dictated perhaps by the need to get around a number of pupils and therefore his lack of time for listening, checking out the pupil's responses, taking account of a broader range of considerations – he seems to make a very rapid assessment of the situation. He commits himself completely to a particular solution to what he perceives to be the pupil's problem, and rides roughshod over a series of signals from the pupil indicating confusion or a contrary view. His talk is all designed to propel her into action. In the process he gives a virtuoso account of the subject's visual character and appeal, in a legitimate attempt to help her 'see' it in a new – perhaps more challenging – way. The approach offers a lot in terms of energizing and motivating the pupil, albeit to carry out the teacher's directions. To the detached observer she didn't appear to be particularly lacking in motivation – she was just not complying with the teacher's agenda for her. There is virtually no attempt to discover or accommodate the pupil's own perceptions, inclinations or feelings, the assumption being that the teacher knows what is required and brings the full force of his considerable personality to bear upon her. She, basically, submits – with good grace. Does she register, even to herself, any sense of reserve or resentment at being coerced?

Clash 1 (16–17)
> *T*: Would it not be better to work straight in colour?
> *P*: No. Most of the work I do at home . . .

Teacher ignores her objection and presses ahead, imposing his own values as well as his own techniques: 'I can see you working there in nice thick paint, straight on . . .'. She gets his drift, adding 'on black paper' – complying.

Clash 2 (52–53)
Pupil runs alongside during his avalanche of suggestion, but has become confused over the meaning, the point of what is being suggested. (In fact she never does get hold of what he *means*, though she is probably capable of *doing* what she's been told.)

> P: Everything messy looks a lot better, doesn't it?
> T: Not necessarily.

He is very clear and adamant – but has he really understood what she is driving at? He doesn't ask – or feel the need to.

Clash 3 (58–61)
She hangs on and tries to insist. 'All thick paint' makes it look 'more realistic' (55): her own piece of theory. He contradicts her with a forceful but distinctly muddy argument, and presses his advantage by ending with a closed question she cannot answer:

> T: What you're doing is . . . You're what? You're doing a . . . ?
> P: Well . . .
> T: You're just doing this as an interpretation . . .

The discussion is drawn away from the work and into the general field of art discourse – the deeply problematic area concerning the relation between the 'realities' of art and life, here muddled by the teacher with the issues of 'realism' or 'naturalism' in painting. The pupil's concept mess = accuracy (a paradox often explored by Impressionist painters) is simply ignored by him.

Clash 4 (63–66)
Not really a clash since she simply accepts his synopsis of her earlier objection in order to refute it comprehensively:

> T: You're saying, 'I'm not doing an interpretation, I'm
>   trying to be realistic.'
> P: Yeah.
> T: Well, you're not.

Nothing at all emerges here of the pupil's powers of sensate ordering, or of the feeling impulse that might be behind the pupil's own expressive act, her seeing.

The upshot of phase 2 was to make plain to us the need to clarify our own ideas about the nature of the expressive/creative dimensions of arts education so that in collaboration with our teacher colleagues we could focus attention where we wanted. Having sorted out our own thinking we then had to find a way of effectively communicating it. Again this was to prove much more difficult than we had imagined. It seemed reasonable to assume that all we were doing was asking teachers to make more deliberate the kind of conversation they often had with their pupils in their everyday encounters with them – spontaneous conversations admittedly but nevertheless concerned to discover the pupil's expressive purposes and the problems confronting them in the execution of those purposes. However, we were beginning to sense that the expressive dimension was rarely the subject of such conversations and that it might not figure as the focus of arts curriculum practice very much either, despite the strong commitment to expression and creativity expressed by teachers in their preliminary discussions with us.

Phase 3

As a consequence of phase 2 we developed a sense both of the nature of the assessment conversation and of its content, and we made the decision to adopt the word 'aesthetic' to describe the principal focus of our interest. Further discussion of this term and the reasons for choosing it follow below. In essence we wished to focus attention upon *meaning*, especially the arousal or engagement of 'cognitive feeling' in the making and in the contemplative enjoyment of a work of art. The term 'aesthetic' was adopted in a deliberate attempt to shift the focus of attention in the assessment conversation away from the technical and on to the semantic dimension of the work. At the beginning of phase 3, we extended our thinking through practising assessment conversations among ourselves and using family and personal friends as volunteers. We then wrote an induction booklet for the project's teachers, setting out our account of aesthetic understanding and providing an 'agenda' for the assessment conversation – which we now began to refer to by the acronym PACT (pupil assessment conversations with teachers). Our booklet offered material and gave direction to the style of conversation we felt would be appropriate for expressive/creative talk to flourish.

The research construct

To investigate talk as a means of assessing a pupil's aesthetic understanding, we devised a research construct which took the form
of an improvised conversation. The research conversation made
equal demands upon the sensing and imagination, and so upon
the subjectivity, of both the teacher and the pupil in the realization
of the meaning and significance of the pupil's art work. Our research
experience suggests to us that the teacher's creative attitude and
personal aesthetic sensitivity may be more critical to the success
of this kind of conversation than her or his subject-specific expertise,
though technical understanding and practical experience of an
art can, of course, prove invaluable in the handling of complex
and sophisticated material. Without an open, flexible approach
to the special demands of the conversation, however, the specialist
skills of the teacher were unavailing, even inhibiting. It goes without
saying that for teacher and pupil to enter upon an improvised
conversation there had to be the possibility of trust and mutual
respect between them.

The topic of the conversation was invariably a particular piece
of art work. In the assessment conversation the teacher was required
to recognize and value the pupil as originator of an authentic image
or performance and respect her responses to what she had made.
The purpose of the conversation was to give the pupil a voice and
allow her space in which to realize, interpret and assess her own
making in a shared act of compassion and contemplation. It should
enable her to interrogate her expressive work and so to test its
validity. The composite act of aesthetic contemplation and reflection is an act of cognition – it is formative. In contemplation the
impulse is recalled, and savoured; the image in reflection is tested,
the expressive achievement compassionately assessed. In consequence, new points of departure are disclosed for further artistic
exploration through the making of meaning, so perpetuating the
cycle that constitutes the arts curriculum.

The assessment conversation was not merely a *viva voce* inter-
rogation of the practicality, the history, of the making process by
oral, retrospective interview. It was not intended as an alternative
to documentation of process; it was to be first an act of construction
and interpretation, and then an act of deliberation and evaluation.
'Reading' a work is constructive of meaning, demanding that the

reader 'make' sense of it. Appraising a work requires deliberation, testing the fit between feeling and form to provide the evidence needed for the final verdict – the pupil's verdict on her own making.

Teachers assisting the project were asked to disregard the instrumental functions of the arts in education – i.e. such considerations as the enhancement of 'life skills', the personalizing of historical information, the acquisition of 'transferable' social and practical skills, moral and philosophical training, all such legitimate and important roles – in order to concentrate specifically and exclusively upon creativity and expression: upon *aesthetic knowing*. Participation in the assessment conversation involved the projection of feeling and imagination, and the exercise of aesthetic judgement by both parties, in a direct interpretation and appraisal of the work. Both partners were to enter the world of the image imaginatively, dwell within it, explore its structure, experience its tensions, respond to its associations, test its strengths, expose its weaknesses – and always in terms of the fit between feeling and form.

The principal rule governing both phases of the reflective encounter was to maintain a living connection between sensing and image. Interpretation and evaluation were to be keyed to the substance of the image – i.e. every interpretive and evaluative statement should find its justification in evidence available within the piece and within the pupil's experience. Aesthetic meaning emerges from the perception of the material presence of the work, as an imaginative construct. The truth against which the work is finally tried resides within its parameters as an expressive project. The assessment conversation begins and ends with the work: is conducted on the 'inside' in imagination and in feeling. The teacher's task is to try to help the pupil 'see' the reality, the import, of her work. Finally teacher and pupil emerge from this close identification with the work to verify and validate its significance in realizing the pupil's expressive purpose. To be clear as to the latter point the pupil must be able to marshal and substantiate her own aesthetic judgements, testing them against what she knows and what she desires.

There was no recommended structure to the assessment conversation, no required procedure. There would always be an element of risk and both partners had to be prepared for failure: each conversation would be unique, each occasion a new beginning.

Experience was to suggest, however, that good conversations usually progress from surface meanings to depth meanings, from engagement with sensate structures to engagement with feelings. Inasmuch as the conversation has a specific focus – the illumination of the aesthetic – it has a relatively precise agenda. It was the teacher's task to draw her or his pupil out and to help her see and appraise her work.

Although we anticipate that the kind of reflective conversation we developed as the project's principal research instrument might profitably be adapted to and adopted within normal school practice, we must stress that the case studies that follow are all, in a sense, experimental. Teachers took time out to talk with pupils at length, in circumstances that could not normally be accommodated within their ordinary teaching programmes. Furthermore, the conversations were observed and recorded by project staff, thus adding to their artificiality. None the less, we feel confident that the insights gained from this research can usefully be incorporated into normal teaching and assessment practices and that we have succeeded in vindicating 'sensible' talk as a rich and revealing medium for the assessment of aesthetic understanding and the enhancement of a pupil's sense of personal integrity and authenticity as an artist.

Conversational talk

The reflective conversation was, then, to be a creative encounter – an aesthetic experience for pupil and teacher alike. The medium of the conversation was talk, employed in an intimate, open, spontaneous, even playful way. The talk would be characterized by intimation as well as proposition; be metaphoric as well as discursive; make use of hints and gestures, speculations and intuitings as well as measured statement of fact and reasoned argument. The good reflective conversation would have all the characteristics of any good conversation. It would be a composition taking shape 'on the wing', achieving focus, cohesion, poignancy in the process. Its eventual success would depend on the ability of the two participants to maintain a creative tension between serious playing and serious work.

The conversation had to be a living experience, fully inhabited by the participants through their talk. The talk would be dynamic in establishing an authentic relationship between the pupil, the teacher and the work. The pupil should not be required merely to recall the practical aspects of the making process as this could very well prove distracting. Instead, she should be led to see the image as the object of a new investigation, of a living act of contemplation. Similarly the teacher had to be prepared for the time being to suspend criticism and judgement derived from external criteria, and open herself or himself up generously and imaginatively to the image, and to the pupil as she responded to her own image.

The teacher might have to work quite hard to set the tone and establish the parameters and the style of the talk. The dynamic of the conversation would rest upon the ability of the pupil and teacher to regard the piece as a living entity, present, in the here and now. Pupil and teacher were to engage in sensing the presence of the piece through talking together. In making, the pupil struggles for a form in the medium with which she is working, to satisfy her feelings and impulses. In the contemplative mode, she attends to the piece, senses its qualities and associations until the feelings it generates take shape, find form, within her. At its best the talk would develop an elasticity and freedom, a playful seriousness which derived from *allowing feeling to work with attention*. When this had been achieved the pupil could feel confident in verifying her image-making and in reflecting upon the quality of her own achievement. The teacher for her part would have valid and reliable qualitative information upon which to base her summative judgement of the pupil's aesthetic progress, needs and potential.

The following information was part of the PACT booklet.

The research agenda

The project had a broad agenda which was concerned to facilitate the pupil's aesthetic understanding. In the research conversation teacher and pupil both respond to the artwork aesthetically. The teacher helps the pupil by drawing her out and helping her to explore and extend her subjective responses and meanings. The following areas were identified as providing useful keys to unlock the pupil's sensing and judgement. Teachers were advised that *they did not constitute a checklist and should not be used as such.* It would not necessarily be appropriate to cover all seven areas in one conversation.

1 The general character or identity of the piece – its presence, sensuality, mood.
2 The structural qualities of the piece – its ordering principle, gestalt, holding form.
3 Its functional efficiency – if the piece has a function, how adequate and how appropriate are design, realization and decoration to the function it is intended to serve?
4 Its artistic and cultural contexts – is the piece good of its kind, considered within the realm of such things?
5 Its symbolic significance – is the piece evocative, powerful, resonant, moving, disturbing?
6 The maker's achievement – does the piece satisfy her? Has her expressive impulse been resolved?
7 The authenticity of the piece – her ownership of it. Does she recognize it as unique and personal, as valid for her?

The success of the conversation would not lie in the *positive* identification of all these elements within the piece. Rather it would lie in the interpretative and evaluative nature of the conversation itself. What discoveries had the participants made? Were they now confident in the judgements made? Was there sufficient evidence to support their judgements?

Towards a good enough conversation

We also offer advice on the way such conversations could be managed with the following hints and suggestions:

1 For the success of the conversation it is essential that the piece in question be 'present', physically, in the form of a recording or as a shared memory.
2 The conversation will succeed best if the teacher
   (a) is genuinely concerned to interpret, understand and develop the pupil's aesthetic understanding;
   (b) is personally engaged in the here and now of the conversation, is curious about the pupil's aesthetic experience and therefore is content to linger, brood and reflect upon this in an open, flexible and friendly way;
   (c) is attentive to the emerging agenda of the pupil and prevents the conversation becoming generalized and circumstantial;
   (d) helps the pupil to identify and reflect upon the expressive

problem (the feeling theme) addressed by the work, and to assess her approach and success;

(e) is prepared to share her or his own aesthetic responses to the piece with the pupil;

(f) avoids interventions that might be interpreted as either threatening or dismissive.

3 The conversation will be in difficulty if the teacher

   (a) remains aloof;
   (b) merely adopts an interrogatory stance towards the pupil;
   (c) encourages the pupil to focus on the history of production;
   (d) relentlessly leads the conversation and is not prepared to improvise, to take risks, to put herself or himself on the line;
   (e) asks closed questions;
   (f) allows the breakdown of trust;
   (g) cannot sympathize or empathize with the pupil;
   (h) invokes only external criteria in judging the work;
   (i) takes notes or makes obvious use of a checklist;
   (j) doesn't listen.

4 The conversation will succeed best if the pupil

   (a) is clear about the purpose and nature of the conversation;
   (b) feels comfortable in the conversation and feels able to talk openly, honestly and confidently about her work;
   (c) feels able to take the initiative in leading the conversation round to the issues she is interested in and concerned about;
   (d) feels ready to formulate and express her own judgement;
   (e) feels personally valued;
   (f) feels that her responses will be accepted as valid;
   (g) does not feel unfairly judged;
   (h) does not feel in competition with her peers;
   (i) is positively drawn out in the interpretive and evaluative process through the contributions and insights offered by the teacher.

5 The conversation may be in difficulties if the pupil

   (a) has nothing to talk about, i.e. impoverished aesthetic experience;
   (b) has little or no experience of talking about her feelings;
   (c) is anxious about the consequences of the conversation;
   (d) has poor verbal communication skills;
   (e) does not feel at ease with or able to trust the teacher or adult expert.

The project pay-off

1 For the pupil:
   (a) a knowing and valuing of what she feels: an expansion of her understanding;
   (b) the achievement of a measure of detachment from and purchase upon her work that allows the development of aesthetic response and judgement in a supportive environment;
   (c) a strengthened sense of ownership of and responsibility for her work;
   (d) the creation of an affective autobiography, i.e. a continuing and unfolding sense of identity;
   (e) an acceptance of the place of her personal, expressive activity and work within the public dimension;
   (f) the possible discovery of new points of departure in her experience of the arts.
2 For the teacher:
   (a) the achievement of the above pupil goals;
   (b) qualitative evidence of the pupil's aesthetic achievement;
   (c) expansion of understanding of the pupil's aesthetic development;
   (d) understanding of the curriculum objectives and assessment practices common to the different arts;
   (e) a balanced 'individualized' curriculum in which production and response alternate in a continuous cycle, governed by each pupil's emergent aesthetic agenda;
   (f) a fully articulated assessment procedure;
   (g) access to the 'inside' of the pupil's aesthetic projects.

To our considerable concern the conversation idea proved difficult to implement. In providing the information in the booklet we hoped to convince the teachers that conversations demanded not simply trust and mutual respect from the participants but a genuine sense of equality in the exchange of information and insights. These conditions, we discovered, could neither be taken for granted nor established simply for the asking. The assessment conversation challenges traditional power structures within the school system (already referred to in the account of phase 1) – but then so does profiling, properly understood. We were optimistic that the special atmosphere generally associated with arts teaching might help to iron out such difficulties.

The phase 3 conversations were something of an improvement upon the previous set, especially in making for a better focus and a more personal approach. In the excerpt that follows, a music teacher, whose phase 2 conversations had been similar to the ones cited above, makes quite a remarkable shift in his approach having read the project induction paper. Here he discusses her composition with an eleventh-year pupil.

[*T* and *P* listen to the pupil's musical composition on tape. There is a very relaxed atmosphere. It is definitely a conversation – both participants are free to speak, interrupt, expand at will, and although *T* has the monopoly on asking questions, one feels that they are both genuinely engaged and interested in the conversation and in each other. There are no embarrassed or awkward silences. *P* is very articulate and confident and enjoys music. *T* and *P* clearly have a good working relationship.]

T: Could you just outline for me the plan that you used for the piece?

P: Well, first of all we put down the chords and the rest of it was actually improvisation over the top of the chords. I was just going to do 1–3–5 chord pattern but   5
we changed it to a different . . . well, that idea actually came from the Hercule Poirot theme, if I remember rightly.

T: Did it? Oh, right. Oh, so that chord idea . . . yeah. So had the idea of the chords come to you through   10
something else?

P: Yeah, um, it was a song – I don't know the name of it – that used C major, A minor, F major and G major the chords.

T: Those are the chords that you used. Yeah?   15

P: And then I changed them, I think, like that C minor. I changed the chords through just sort of playing about with the piano and they came to me and then, um, I was playing Hercule Poirot and then we decided to put that in it as well and it came round, so . . .   20

T: What was the thing about this Hercule Poirot thing . . . this is the idea I suppose, yeah?

P: Yeah.

T: Think back to before, how come you used it? Did you

just sit down at the piano and think, 'That's quite nice,   25
I'll try and play that'?

P: Yeah, I tend to listen to TV programmes . . .

T: Yeah.

P: . . . and try, if I like the tune, I tend to try and work them
out. Like, I've done one of the Agatha Christie titles – I   30
don't know what it is – I played about with that. Oh,
yeah, Miss Marples. And I quite liked the idea of trying
to work out Hercule Poirot on the piano and did it by
ear.

T: Right, so it wasn't necessarily first of all an idea for a   35
composition?

P: No, it wasn't. Not first of all.

T: It was just, 'I like that'?

P: Yeah.

T: 'I like that, I'll try and play it and find out what it was   40
on the piano'?

P: Yeah.

T: What was it about that musical idea that appeals to
you?

P: Well, I don't know, I think it was just unusual. I sort of   45
tried it . . . Because a lot of my music is sort of always in
C major or something like that I decided to try
something different, you know, sort of try and make
it unusual in a way. But, no, it just seemed to fit
together and . . .   50

T: Is it the sound that's . . . ?

P: Yeah, I think . . .

T: Unusual?

P: Yeah, I think the sound altogether fitted together.

T: What makes it unusual? Can you describe . . . ? This is   55
the hard thing. Even if it's in technical terms, you know,
that . . .

P: I think it's the arrangement of the chords, 'cos they're
all minors. I changed them from major to minor.

T: Yeah, that's interesting, because you get a different   60
sound if it's major or minor.

P: Yeah, it sounds sad in places and then where you've
got the fast bit in the middle it's all cheer . . . sort of . . .

T: It's that idea that initially struck me, because when I
    heard it, and when you must have played it to me, I   65
    thought first of all, I thought, 'That's a nice idea.' But
    we can't sing it because it's in two or three parts, but it's
    that [sings and mimes] na-num, na-num. You know,
    that sort of . . . sound.

P: Yeah, I think the voice helped it as well. Using that, er,   70
    well, it was a vibrating voice, wasn't it? It also had
    eerieness, I suppose.

T: That sequence of chords then, obviously that's the
    one you thought of, that you arrived at, so you feel
    quite happy with that. It's quite satisfying. [P is   75
    nodding and saying 'yes' throughout this.] Does that
    come again . . . ? Does that affect the piece later on?

P: It does because it's still all in the same key.

T: The tempo changes, you see . . .

P: [interrupts] The tempo changes but the chords stay   80
    the same.

T: Right. Is that satisfying, do you think?

P: Well, yes, because in a way it actually changes the
    dimensions of the chords because it sounded different
    when we speeded it up . . .   85

T: [interrupts] Because the . . .

P: [interrupts] Tempo had speeded up. It changed the
    effect. Because at the beginning it was quite eerie
    and then it cheered up, it sort of . . .

T: Yeah, yeah. So in fact a different . . . So if you use   90
    one set of chords at the beginning, if you use this idea at
    the beginning and then change to another set of
    chords in the middle . . . What do you think about that,
    as opposed to what you did?

P: [small pause, thinking] I think that would change the   95
    overall effect of it.

T: So it's a sort of . . . What are you aiming for?

P: It'd have to fit in. It would have to be similar sort of
    chords, I think, to fit in.

T: The overall effect you're aiming for is one of [long   100
    pause, searching for the appropriate word, gesturing] . . .
    coherence, then?

P: Yeah.

T: Does it feature later on?

P: Yes, it features right at the end as well. We've got it   105
at the beginning and the end. So it's like a jam
sandwich, if you like.

T: Oh, yeah. Go on, tell me a bit more about that.

P: Well, it's like a jam sandwich because we've got the
beginning of it and it's sort of slow and then it picks   110
up in the middle and then it goes back to being slow
and ends.

T: That's a common enough sort of musical structure
then, isn't it?

P: Yeah, that's why I call it a jam sandwich.   115

T: Ah, I see. It's two slices of bread with jam in the middle.
Right. Ah, I've got it. Yeah.

T: If you were to listen to the piece, what sort of features
do you think stand out as being the sort of most
satisfying to yourself? I mean, overall I presume   120
you're quite satisfied with it?

P: Yeah, I think . . . I like the middle bit the best out of all
of it because . . .

T: [interrupts] Yeah, why's that?

P: I don't know. It stands out more as the picked up beat   125
but the beginning and the end seem to sort of round
it off and make it . . . but . . .

T: This 'picking up the beat', can you just expand on
that a bit?

P: Um, it changed the dimensions slightly but it kept the   130
same sort of feeling. I don't know.

T: This is back to the chords then, is it, sort of thing?

P: Yeah.

T: That's the thing that . . .

P: But the improvisation on top, that was just, sort of,   135
have a go and see what happens, basically.

This is a genuine exchange between equals – there is no sense
of the teacher's dominant status here despite his insistent questioning, or of the need to hurry on to production. They linger. He
is obviously motivated by genuine interest in and understanding
of the piece under discussion, and commitment to the pupil and

her project. He pushes her to help him understand – to articulate both the process of composition (including the frank identification of the inspiration of the piece) and her sense of the structure and meaning of the piece. She is convincing about her satisfaction with what she has made and provides ample evidence of the operation of quite advanced musical 'understanding'. The teacher provides sufficient emotional support to allow her to feel confident in her search for understanding and adequate ways of communicating with him – he is often 'playful' in his engagement with the piece – and yet does not crowd or impose upon her, leaving her plenty of space to develop and present her thoughts and feelings. The discussion is focused upon the art work more or less throughout and upon her experiences in respect of it. That having been said, might she not have been encouraged to expand upon the feeling/expressive aspect of the piece? We don't really learn much more than that it had 'a certain feeling' and later that she found its overall coherence satisfying. The teacher senses an opportunity in her reference (125–127) to 'picking up the beat' but he can only respond by talking about the 'changed dimension'.

Our difficulties with the expressive/creative area – what we were now calling the 'aesthetic' – persisted. Despite our agenda of issues to be discussed and our warning Do's and Don'ts (in the PACT document) concerning the handling of the conversation, it was rather the exception than the rule that the conversations managed to penetrate to the inside of the pupil's expressive act.[1] We were going to have to think again about how people might set about looking together at a work of art and what kind of language might facilitate such looking. We were also becoming aware that the conversation, when it worked, fell almost naturally into two parts; it certainly had two discernibly different dimensions. On the one hand the participants spent time uncovering, discovering, even recovering the image in all its power to evoke feelings, emotions, associations and meanings – in its power to signify, its 'presence' (presentness). On the other hand, there was an irresistible tendency at some point (or points) to weigh the worth of the work, to pronounce oneself satisfied or dissatisfied in respect of this particular feature or that: to deliver a verdict even. Essentially this was a judgement by the maker herself upon what she had made; a public judgement delivered in the presence of the other participant, possibly corroborated, possibly not. Contemplation followed by reflection.

Furthermore, we were becoming increasingly interested in the idea of contemplative reflection itself – increasingly clear that the composite act of contemplation and reflection was in itself a creative act and that the insight it could deliver and the changes in perception it could provoke were every bit as valuable and as powerful from the educational point of view as making – the dominant modality in arts education. Although it was clear that PACT had considerable potential in terms of formative assessment within making, as a form of contemplative reflection it seemed a skill in its own right and a dimension of arts education ripe for development: appraisal as the counterpart of the making of meaning, the two modes constituting between them the twin aspects of the arts curriculum.

Phase 4

All these matters were the subject of further discussion with the pilot schools, with whom we had now been working for the best part of a year. We decided to have one more go at communicating our idea to teachers in the final months remaining to us. This time we thought we ought to take on an entirely new set of schools and so, after a brief period of negotiation, we arranged to work with four new schools during November and December 1990. The original induction booklet was revamped and additional material, including exemplary video tapes, prepared for a full day's practical induction course. The documentary material was sent to the teachers in advance. On the day, an opening discussion session spent exploring and explaining the position papers was followed by a practical session in which the teachers participated in assessment conversations, in the role of 'pupil'. That is to say, the teachers were asked to bring along some of their own art work and members of the project team attempted to draw them into assessing creativity in a reflective conversation. On the whole these practical sessions seemed to go well. By the end of the day four of the five schools invited to attend the day were well satisfied with what was being proposed and we parted in keen anticipation of the collaboration to come.

The results from phase 4 were, however, similar to those from phase 3. The teachers on the whole felt the conversations had been worth while – many went further and were thoroughly enthusiastic about talking to their pupils in this particular way, wishing that there were more such opportunities within their normal day-to-day teaching. However, they also raised the by now familiar objection that these kinds of conversation, no matter how desirable in theory, were totally impossible in practice since they were so demanding of teachers' time. To concentrate in this way upon individual pupils was only possible at the expense of the rest of the class. Most of our teachers saw no prospects for what we were suggesting within the realities of schooling as they knew it. They also warned us that the ethos of our approach seemed to contradict the National Curriculum and the new 'quantitative' emphasis in assessment. We shall take up both these points later. There was also hesitancy and confusion over not simply what we meant by the aesthetic but over locating the expressive within children's work and then finding anything very much to say about it. Where some kind of headway was made – and all was not a blank – then teachers regularly expressed considerable surprise not simply at the amount children found and indeed wanted to say about their work, but also at the quality and perceptiveness of what was said. They were by no means lost for words. The teachers were genuinely taken aback. All this again seemed to confirm that we had a valuable resource here if only we could make it work.

Writing up

The resources for the fieldwork phase of the project (15 months) came to an end and we began to analyse in detail the data collected: audio and video tapes, transcripts of meetings, seminars and interviews as well as journal notes from observations. The feedback to the teachers at the end of each phase was consistent with our critical inquiry approach to the research – problematizing the issues of both the aesthetic and assessment and addressing challenging questions with our teacher collaborators.

In some respects it seemed as if we had made nothing like the progress we had been hoping for. We had been unable, reliably, to identify with the teachers the area of aesthetic experience we were interested in. We had not reliably trained anyone to conduct a fully effective conversation. No doubt this was partly because we did not ourselves know what we wanted, which had been the reason for the inductive approach to the research. It is as a result of detailed analysis of the pupil–teacher interactions that make up the substantive part of the writing up of the research that we now sense what might make a fairer, more effective induction programme. We hope that the assessment strategy made explicit in the account that follows might make a practical contribution to the subject we set out to investigate.

3

THEORETICAL

The arts curriculum cycle

The notion of the 'aesthetic' is sometimes unjustly dismissed from educational discussion either as belonging to abstract philosophical discourse or as culturally high-falutin: some divine state of grace granted only to the most sensitive and refined of souls, beyond comment or criticism by ordinary mortals. We have not found this view helpful to our understanding of children's subjective experiencing in the arts. The 'aesthetic', to our understanding, is not so much the reward of some esoteric practice or a blessing bestowed upon a chosen few but rather a mode of cognition, a way of knowing: it is not a condition of being, but a process, an operation, a way of engaging with the world, a form of work. *We do not experience the aesthetic so much as experience aesthetically.* Thus we talk about aesthetic *knowing*, aesthetic *responding*, aesthetic *perceiving*, aesthetic *understanding*; all these are constructive and constitutive activities, ways of becoming as well as ways of being.

We have turned, in systematizing our observations of aesthetic development and of learning in the arts, to Rom Harré and his book, *Personal Being* (1983). He attaches importance for personal

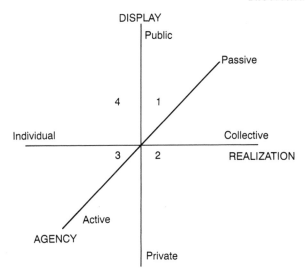

Figure 2 A social reality matrix.
Source: After Harré (1983).

development to the expressive dimension of human behaviour, through what he calls 'identity projects'. Harré's appeal to us is his emphasis on the *processes* of individual growth rather than upon the outcomes in terms of products or artefacts. In his model the several dimensions of experience are dynamically interrelated. In accordance with this view of identity, our thinking focuses precisely upon *the development of the pupil and not the fate of the product.* As we have already said, we see aesthetic education contributing crucially to the development of individual identity, especially to that sense we may have of one's expressive and creative self at the core of being.

Harré proposes three dimensions to social reality: public/private *display*, individual/collective *realization* and active/passive *agency*. He represents them as a matrix (see Figure 2).

Harré suggests that personal 'development' occurs as an unceasing sequence of 'identity projects' involving a clockwise circling around the matrix from quadrant 1 to quadrant 4 and on to quadrant 1 again. He describes the four transitions as an invariant sequence of operations:

conventionalization → appropriation → transformation → publication → conventionalization

Reducing the model to two dimensions (Figure 3) provides us with

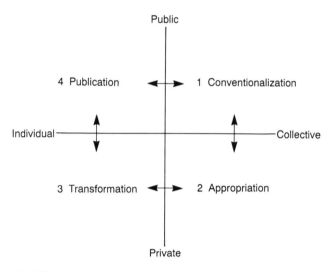

Figure 3   The arts curriculum cycle.

the means of mapping both productive and contemplative aesthetic activities (Harré's third dimension: agency).

An assessment profile in the arts would need to allow for graduated attainments in respect of each of the four operations and in terms of production and contemplation. Such a scheme could be developed quite quickly based upon the witness of experienced teachers. A further research project would be needed, however, to test, modify and elaborate it.

Each transitional operation becomes the focus of curriculum provision at every stage of the child's aesthetic development. Converting Harré's four operations into 'aesthetic' formulations, i.e. into statements applicable to arts education, we arrive at four aspects of the pupil's aesthetic understanding:

1 The conventionalization of aesthetic understanding.
2 The appropriation of aesthetic understanding.
3 The transformation of aesthetic understanding.
4 The publication of aesthetic understanding.

The model we are about to elaborate is a cyclical, process model: the sequence runs from quadrant 1 to quadrant 4 and then begins again. It applies to both artistic production and contemplative activity. It may also be used to map reflection. At every phase there is a degree of reciprocity between adjacent quadrants. As we have said already, we are focusing precisely upon the aesthetic development of the pupil and only dealing with the fate of the product in so far as it affects and illuminates that development, and this is consonant with our earlier statement concerning the arts curriculum and personal or individual development. These ideas now need elaborating.

Conventionalization

This quadrant of the model is both the beginning and the end of an unceasing cycle – the process of problem formulation and resolution in the arts that Harré designates 'identity projects'. All expression derives from and draws upon the cultural stock, upon tradition. The child is born into a cultural matrix and must first establish herself there – accommodate to the phenomena of art, embodied in rules and conventional forms. The pupil's feeling responses – her sensate orderings – must first find expression within the general discourse of feeling as conventionalized by the culture. Then in terms of her own emergent identity, having published herself and submitted herself to praise, having proposed a role for herself, she must be granted the right to participate (to transact and traffic) in what Oakeshott (1977) called 'the conversation of mankind'.[2] This she will do within and by means of the conventions available, conventions that are constantly under review and subject to alteration, substitution and degradation as the culture protects and renews itself. The child's products and responses are offered as additions to the conventional wisdom of society, and she herself becomes a bearer of the culture, a transmitter, a reformer, a guardian. She comes to perceive herself as authentic, as a maker-of-meanings among other such makers – as a member of the wedding.

It is in this sense that the arts are about personal development. Knowing, which comes perhaps as a flash of inspiration, a moment of enlightenment, an intuition, an intimation in the process of transformation, and is verified in the process of publication, is now realized as viable behaviour, available as a form for the management of feeling, as a construct for the ordering and elaboration of the life of feeling within the public world. This is the practical benefit of an experience recognized and cherished primarily for the distinctive pleasure it gives us – a pleasure we are correctly inclined to imbue with much richer, even spiritual, values. To know aesthetically is to know yourself as transcendent and yet grounded at the same time, corporeality being at once our curse and our blessing. It is only by our fruits – by the fruits in this case of our aesthetic understanding, i.e. our individual aesthetic judgements – that we are known and may take our place in the community of public discourse. What governs that discourse is a set of principles, aesthetic principles that provide aesthetic judgement with its basis in reason (i.e. its 'reasonableness') and the possibility of a sense of order.

Appropriation

Feelings arise in a cultural context. They find expression and realization in ways and by means available in and acceptable (meaningful) to that culture. We appropriate the conventions available within our culture for the expression of personal feeling, for the transaction and communication of personal meaning. It is clearly of the utmost importance that children should be schooled in such forms, customs, conventions and practices as will permit and facilitate the legitimate expression of feeling. Much of such 'schooling' goes on outside the school itself through processes of 'natural' or informal socialization and acculturation, but often much remains to be done if the individual child is to have access to the means of expression she needs to live a balanced, full and healthy emotional life. It is also reasonable to expect schools to extend such awareness and such opportunities way beyond what might be acquired casually, given the resources available in our society for extending children's knowledge and experience and for accelerating development and compensating for deficit. Children should be given the opportunity to appropriate the expressive forms they need from the full range now available in the modern world, both contemporary and traditional, and to convert them into a personal style, signature or voice.

Transformation

Transformation is the creative search for personal knowledge through the representation of feeling impulse in images 'closer to the heart's desire'. The pupil's aesthetic project is an identity project in this particular sense, its main purpose being the representation of sensate experience in imagery that is unique, particular and owned.

Schools seem only weakly to appreciate the full import of this aspect of arts education, despite the prominence given to the production of art work and, supposedly, to the pupil's 'personal' imagery. The transformative principle applies not only to the pupil's feelings but also to the conventions available for their expression and, of course, to the pupil's sense of individuality. As has already been said, for work to be genuinely transformative, the teacher must be able to identify (and identify with) the pupil's aesthetic intention, i.e. with her creative–expressive action by means of which feeling and medium fuse in a process that transforms both. The teacher may not directly enter these private worlds of appropriation and transformation. Her only access is through the child's acts of Publication and Conventionalization. But then the teacher must find a way of comprehending the personal expressive character of the work so as to be able to supply her own responses to the work. She must, however, be able to see, to hear what is going on for the pupil in the work, and the pupil can help her do so.

Since understanding appropriation and transformation lies at the heart of good arts teaching, we elaborate upon it more fully in Chapter 4 in the analysis of pupil–teacher talk. In particular we try to demonstrate that the pupil's essentially private acts of sensate ordering may indeed be located, identified and evaluated in public discussion with the teacher. We shall show how the aesthetic response is constituted of observable 'feeling ideas', of palpable structures or elements which embody and convey the feeling dimension of the work. By taking sensate ordering as evidence of intelligent feeling, of aesthetic understanding, we remove assessment from the domain of the teacher's personal preference and key it firmly into the pupil's perception of her own performance. Assessment thereby transcends the mere grunt of satisfaction, the dumb hunch, the feeling in the gut. Teachers can learn to concentrate upon discovering the character of the pupil's sensate ordering, i.e. her capacity for making meaning in the arts. The child's underlying, even unconscious, world of feeling (her particular loves, hates and obsessions, i.e. all that is strictly private) safely remain her own business. Teaching need not be intrusive. But *evidence* of transformation is available if the teacher knows how and where to look for it.

Publication

The publication of feeling and hence its social ratification and validation is the destiny of, in fact constitutes a reasonable definition of, expression in the arts. Contrary to the stereotype, the expressive impulse is in fact unsatisfied in us until the work is placed in the public domain, albeit anxiously and with some trepidation, as an effort of communication with and an invitation to validation by others. The work will then be judged in terms of its power to sustain aesthetic contemplation. It is in this special act of public sharing – especially through the neglected dimension of creative and imaginative talk – that pupil and teacher foster publication together. The teacher is the pupil's first (and privileged) public. They meet in Winnicott's (1971) 'potential space' and on very special terms – as we shall see in Chapter 4. It is in the pupil's act of publication that the teacher is able to connect with the work, provide support and make appropriate and relevant formative assessments. As with conventionalization, appropriation and transformation, we have more to say about publication in the case studies below, since our understanding of all these concepts has largely evolved from that process. It is in publication that feeling becomes judgement – where the so-called aesthetic emotions manifest themselves: wonder, awe, reverence, delight.

Teachers instinctively wish to reward their pupils with public praise and acknowledgement, indeed many arts teachers see this kind of personal endorsement as perhaps the only contribution they can make to their pupil's development. Praise is indeed the principal duty of the teacher as first-perceiver of the pupil's work. Formative assessment will only work if it is non-judgemental, even celebratory. For the teacher's endorsement of the pupil to carry any weight the pupil must feel that the teacher has been able to grasp the direction, character and thrust of the creative and expressive experience she has undergone. Where the teacher's endorsement seems alien to the pupil's own experience of appropriation and transformation, publication is robbed of its formative power.

The assessment conversation as we have come to appreciate it involves an imaginative interpretation (apprehension) of the art work and the exercise of judgement in reflection. Through the act of reflection the whole cycle of the pupil's aesthetic experience may be reviewed.

Another way of looking

Aesthetic and non-aesthetic responses

In today's technological society, where the highest regard is often given to positivistic thought and propositional language, the potential for aesthetic understanding and communication is not generally fostered, even through arts education. Schools, as social institutions, are designed to be influential in perpetuating the dominant value system. As a consequence of the high value that is placed on functional and rational modes of organizing experience, the aesthetic response as a way of knowing tends to be underdeveloped and is wrongly believed to be purely and simply private and feelingful and not to involve the public processes of thought, reflection and evaluation. The public status of art in education is correspondingly low.

The aesthetic response is not synonymous with the response to art. It is perfectly possible and, indeed often more usual, to respond to the arts non-aesthetically. It is helpful here, therefore, to distinguish between aesthetic and non-aesthetic responses. In the present political climate the distinction is an important one since it might be argued that the aesthetic response is in some sense inherently subversive. It is important too when we examine the material we have collected as a result of asking teachers to talk to pupils about their arts work.

When we attend to an object non-aesthetically we tend to employ re-cognitive rather than cognitive strategies: we seek its relevance and fittingness to the concepts we bring to it. So, for instance, we might look at a painting, identify its subject matter ('Ah, a lily pond!') and, satisfied, move on. Confronted with an unfamiliar style or representation, we might need to linger a little longer and adjust our preconceptions ('A jumble of random lines? A nose, an eye, a mouth? Ah, a face!'). Our perception will, however, tend to stop at recognition, on achievement of the predetermined goal. This kind of perception tends to be economical and functional; it involves a reduction of the incoming data to match pre-existing schemata in the interest of recognition. Perception is subject to the perceiver's non-aesthetic intentions.

With this kind of functional attention, the sensuous and structural aspects of the object – its 'surface' – will be largely redundant and tend to be ignored where they do not contribute to the recognitive intention. When we perceive aesthetically, however, the very excess of these aspects becomes the focus of interest and attention. We focus upon the surface texture of the work, becoming absorbed in it in a desire to explore, savour and get to know its sensuous and expressive qualities and their significance. In the sense that it allows us to 'lose ourselves' in the act of contemplation, this way of attending is quite literally *disinterested*. It may include but goes beyond mere 'reading'.

We have found Rosamund Osbourn's (1988) research into visual aesthetic responses to works of art extremely valuable to our own study, in particular her careful contextual account of aesthetic knowing and her use of personal construct theory as an analytical instrument. As she describes it, the aesthetic response is constructive, requiring 'a positive input of energy'. It is characterized by a willingness to entertain confusion, ambiguity and contradiction and to seek expansion in further material and stimulation.

The differences between aesthetic and non-aesthetic perception are further clarified when one considers what count as the satisfactory outcomes in each case. For non-aesthetic perception, satisfaction is achieved by closure – the straightforward matching of solution to enquiry – while for aesthetic perception, satisfaction is to be derived from the maintenance of investigative activity: 'a constantly circling wholeness and lack of consummatory climax'. Satisfaction therefore resides more in a 'trend of behaviour than in any specific end result' (Osbourn 1988: 125). Children often require considerable support in achieving satisfactory strategies of contemplation.

Clearly there are implications for assessment here. Traditional assessment practices would conform to the reductive tendency of non-aesthetic engagement, by predetermining the knowledge that the pupil shall show evidence of. The pupil selects from her experience in order to fit the function of the question she is asked. Where questions function to make rigorous selection and particular ordering of experience a necessity for the one who answers, it is perhaps little wonder that the more open and active form of aesthetic knowing should have evaded traditional assessment criteria and even been judged unassessable.

Osbourn's phrase, 'trend of behaviour', helped us in analysing the data upon which our insights are based. The data are in the form of talk between adults with experience in the arts and school pupils.

If we understand talk as behaviour we can begin to differentiate between its different forms and purposes and to relate these to our growing understanding of aesthetic response. We can begin to distinguish those forms of talk which are non-aesthetic in their orientation – which are functional and tend towards closure – from those which evade or exceed such categorization, excite and engage aesthetic knowing and yield intrinsic satisfactions.

Language and aesthetic response

The research conversations have been analysed with two dimensions in mind. In the first place we are looking for evidence that the pupil's aesthetic understanding has been aroused and that the work under scrutiny can function as the site of intelligent feeling and of sensibility at work. At the same time we have been examining the dynamics of the conversation, looking at the types of language used by the participants, the nature and bearing of their personal relationship and the quality of the experience engendered through talk. This second dimension has proved richly interesting and scarcely separable from the first.

In examining occasions on which pupils are talking about their unique and individual engagement we have noticed a particular kind of language in operation – more tentative, less conclusive, but often carrying more conviction than that which they use in response to a closed line of questioning or a purely technical enquiry. And where coherent talk breaks down, it is often supplemented by eloquent gesture. This, we have come to feel, is language used aesthetically, at times even poetically, both to generate and to convey understanding.

Reading what others have written about the arts and language, it seems that we are not alone in the observations we have made. Lesley Perry (1984), in an essay entitled 'The arts, judgment and language', distinguishes between two forms of communication open to individuals. In the public world there is standard and conventional communication, 'a *generalising* thing' based on the idea of resemblance between individuals. And there is private communication by which the individual both tests linguistic meanings (*appropriates* them rather than merely accepting them as standard) and uses them to articulate an inner state of mind. He argues that these forms are not neatly separated but overlap to varying degrees according to the specific context of language use.

In the case studies that follow (Chapter 4), language frequently tends towards the 'private' kind. The speaker struggles to realize her or his meaning, her or his particular and unique sensing, but within a form of language that will be recognized and responded to by the conversation partner. There is a tension between personal discovery of significance through speech and the need to share, to converse, and thus, inevitably, to orientate towards the other person's point of view. The conversation partner plays an important role in determining the mode in which the pupil is permitted to operate; whether she or he is free to use the emergent meanings of private speech or is bounded by an expectation that meanings should be finished and public (i.e. that there are 'correct' or 'wrong' answers). To state this another way: whether the pupil is permitted to respond aesthetically or non-aesthetically. Perry writes:

> Aesthetic experience is very much personal and often uniquely so in its origins, and it shares the general difficulty that arises whenever an individual, utilizing the generalising medium of language, wants to communicate what is peculiar to him to others and to make them aware of his inner state.
>
> (Perry 1984: 23)

As we have done, Perry locates the arts 'in the borderland of articulation' (i.e. between the public and the private domains of speech) where 'the pressure on language becomes extreme'. It is precisely here that our conversations have their place; between the purely public and private polarities of the process model, between transformation and conventionalization – i.e. in Publication.

The Russian linguist and psychologist, L. S. Vygotsky (1972) also distinguishes two forms of speech resembling those described by Perry. The very individualized activity of 'inner' (private) speech is characterized by abbreviation and the condensation of meaning, the use of idioms and predicates which appear, in comparison to 'external' (public) speech, 'disconnected and incomplete'.

There are occasions, says Vygotsky, when external speech comes to resemble inner speech; this is when both speakers know what is going on, when their thoughts coincide or are sufficiently orientated towards one another. The private use of speech (inner speech) can be nurtured by a context that is sympathetic to its use. The case studies certainly show that where conversation partners achieve a closeness of understanding, where they begin to establish a rapport, the distinction between inner and outer, private and public speech begins to blur (e.g. case study 5). Intimacy leads to intimation, to aesthetic response.

In our conversations – in aesthetic talk – intimacy is achieved through the shared contemplation of the art work. As we discuss below, this sharing is crucial to our notion of publication and of praise. The quality of the speakers' attentiveness to the art work is witnessed by language that adapts itself to the particularities of the object addressed, and to the particularities of present time and present place – by utterances, gestures, the responses of the other speaker.

Aesthetic understanding manifests itself in – and *as* – a complex, multiple, dynamic, contingent and 'always recent' (Perry 1984: 29) response. Each utterance changes the context of which the arts object is, in this sense, a 'living' part. Public forms of language (the purest form is writing: out of time, final draft, immutable) tend to militate against such fluidity. According to Vygotsky one of the main semantic peculiarities distinguishing inner (private) speech from external (public) speech is 'the preponderance of the *sense* of a word over its *meaning*'. Sense is

> a dynamic, fluid, complex whole, which has several zones of unequal stability. Meaning is only one of the zones of sense, the most stable and precise zone. A word acquires its sense from the context in which it appears; in different contexts it changes sense. Meaning remains stable throughout the changes of sense . . . The sense of a word . . . is a complex, mobile, protean phenomenon; it changes in different minds and situations and is almost unlimited.
>
> (Vygotsky 1972: 146)

Publication admits both an act of shared contemplation, where language has the quality of sense, and a shared act of critical reflection, where language is dominated by meaning.

Searching talk for evidence of aesthetic understanding

In order systematically to explore the two related dimensions that correspond roughly to the content and the form of the conversations we had to devise a framework that would allow us to identify, distinguish and evaluate the various elements in which we were interested. It made sense to tie the analysis to the conceptual matrix developed to describe the arts curriculum. The four operations identified in the model now become the principal categories for sorting the data contained in the conversations. An example of how this was done is shown below.

The transformation category needs particular explanation. Our analysis here is based upon Kelly's (1955) theory of personal constructs, which Osbourn summarises as follows:

> In Personal Construct Theory interest centres upon the individual and upon his interaction with the world *as he interprets it*. Through the application of a personal repertoire of bi-polar constructs, an individual structures his world, conceptualises and interprets it and, on the basis of judgements made, seeks to anticipate events. Polar adjectives such as 'strong–weak' and 'big–small', or even polar phrases such as 'the jagged quality of the hills set against the sky' versus 'the smooth, flowing quality of the water', reflect the dichotomous abstractions upon which judgement is based. Construct theory is concerned with the way in which these are organised and interconnected.
>
> By means of this structural network a system is established which enables an individual to codify and give meaning to his experience. This is constantly tested and adapted, in order to perfect a more effective interaction with the world, by a process which allows useful constructs to be retained and strengthened, whilst ineffective ones are either modified or discarded.
>
> (Osbourn 1988: 194)

Transformation, it will be remembered, is the reciprocal engagement of feeling and form. It is the modification of the medium by the expressive impulse, and of the impulse by the resistance offered to it in the process of embodiment in the medium. Evidence of the transformational operation – the structuring of feeling and form – is revealed in *sensate constructs* that constitute the surface texture or qualities of the work and that hold the key to apprehending the work's aesthetic meaning, its imaginative significance.

Following Osbourn we distinguish between sensate *surface* and sensate *depth* in a work of art. Here we have in mind the way sensuous constructs operate simultaneously as ways of ordering meaning at the level of direct attention (primary perception) and, metaphorically, as ways of evoking imaginative (depth) meanings. So, for example, cool colours and warm colours may be contrasted at the surface to constitute one aspect of the *body* of the work while at the same time evoking a mood or atmosphere, an imaginative ambience. It is the direct experience of this fusion, this oscillation of attention between surface and depth, form and feeling, that constitutes what we mean by the experience of aesthetic understanding – the aesthetic response. The sensate surface will include every appeal to sensory apprehension offered by the work. Colours, for example, may be strong/weak; shapes, concave/convex; light, dim/brilliant; lines, heavy/light; movements, sudden/slow; smell, pungent/bland; texture, rough/smooth. 'Surface' will also include other elements, such as story or narrative material, the traces left by certain techniques and instruments, the use of conventional formulae – in short, surface is everything we see, touch or hear that constitutes the body and articulates the structure of the piece. Depth is the operation of those self-same sensate structures to evoke and order feeling. Depth identifies that sense we have of the 'presence' of a piece. If surface delights us, depth is what moves us.

For a work to evoke imaginative meanings, to have what we call 'depth', one must have apprehended its surface, picked up its sensate qualities, its structural order. Depth is cognition operating upon perception; its meaning is connotative; it is the realm of imagination, of mood, character, symbol, metaphor, resonance. Depth meaning (or, as Vygotsky would have it, 'sense') is generated across fields of knowledge. When a work is explored as depth, then memory, sensing, imagination, personal associations, intuition, dream and cultural inheritances begin to inter-weave, to create an increasingly dynamic, volatile and mesmerizing texture of significance and experience; the personality, ambience, distinctive flavour of the piece emerges; its 'feel', its 'real presence' (Steiner 1989) for those contemplating or enjoying it.

Aesthetic development or maturation in terms of transformation occurs as development of the ability to respond to the growing complexity and intensity of the way surface yields to depth, not by becoming more transparent, more separate, but by becoming more opaque, more self-sufficient, more fused. The mature aesthetic understanding is increasingly obsessed with and satisfied by surface-as-depth, experienced as unresolved and inexhaustible. The perception of depth is the condition of disinterested interest and distanced attachment that characterizes mature aesthetic judgement.

One final observation will be made and our account of the analytical framework is complete. Constructs are made in respect of what Kelly calls 'elements'. These are the concepts, constituent factors or conventional features of a particular art form; in music, for instance, rhythm, tone, harmony, tune, tempo. The greater the pupil's awareness of the range of sensate material available in respect of the different elements that characterize a particular art form, the richer will be her experience of depth in the making process and of depth in aesthetic contemplation. Again, as we have indicated earlier, Osbourn's research has been very helpful as we have sought a systematic method of analysing our own data. She too used talk in exploring her subjects' aesthetic responses.

In the example that follows we illustrate our analytic method. 'Spreadsheets' like Table 1 were used to investigate the constructs systematically and in particular to disclose the evidence to support reasoned judgements or assessments of the pupil. The procedure proved to be useful in unpacking 'transformation'. This brief extract is taken from the analysis of case study 7 (next chapter).

M: If we look at the picture, what bits of the picture do
   you feel happiest with, do you like best?

J: Um . . . I like these bits down at the bottom, where you can
   see the water and the rocks, and there's dark shadows
   in the water. Um . . . and I like it where, here where   5
   there's, um, like it's a sheer drop, it's straight down . . .
   and you can actually see that [points to a 'stack' of
   rock rising sheer out of the water]. And usually I'm not
   very good at drawing those things . . . Uh . . . I also like this
   bit up here where . . . um [Points up to the left hand   10
   side of the picture. He was originally pointing down to the
   bottom right. He's pointing up now to the sort of middle
   left where there is a high cliff face.] . . . where there is a
   contrast between the jagged rocks and the grass and
   the earth and the shrubs up at the top, which are on . . .   15
   like the hill.

M: Is it the feel of it or, or the colours you've got, or, or the
   shapes of it, or, or because you really feel you've
   caught, you know, that, that contrast?

J: I feel I've caught that contrast, yeah, between . . . the . . .   20
       browny nice greeny, browny earthy colour and the grey
       . . . rock face.

Table 1   Example 'spreadsheet' used in the analysis

Line nos	Elements	Transformation constructs	
		Surface	*Depth*
3–9	2D surface: 'these bits at the bottom'	water vs not water rocks vs not rocks shadows vs not shadows	
9–16	2D surface: 'this bit up here'	jagged rocks vs grass, earth, shrubs	(mixed feelings)
19–21	colour	greeny, browny, earthy colour vs grey rock face	(mixed feelings)

In the opening section (lines 3–9) Jack happily attends to the representational elements in his painting. He is pleased with the way he has rendered rock, water and shadow and points them out happily and confidently to his conversation partner (publication). His approval of what he has done signals ownership (conventionalization). He confides his lack of drawing skills (appropriation). In the next section (9–16) the representational elements are similarly pointed out and the painting approved of. He offers the concept 'contrast', which indicates both appropriation and depth (the structure carries conflicting feeling). The third section (19–21) shifts from representational features to more purely sensate elements (colour). Again the feeling and form of the contrast are noted by Jack and he is confident of his achievement as a painter. He expresses a certain personal pleasure in 'the nice greeny, browny, earthy colour' that, later in the conversation, transforms into a strong depth construct carrying much of the imaginative meaning of the piece (see case study 7 below).

Although the categories above are a useful tool for understanding the data, they do not on their own reflect the overall sense of integration.

The first principle in music hearing is not, as many people presume, the ability to distinguish the separate elements in a composition and recognise its devices, but to experience the primary illusion, to feel the consistent movement and recognise at once the commanding form which makes this piece *an inviolable whole*. Even young children can do this when they listen delightedly to a tune.

(Langer 1953)

There is no content to the conversations that is not part of the language in which it is expressed. The medium is, in this sense, also the message (just as the meaning of a dance is not to be abstracted from its realized living form). The aesthetic focus of the conversation is embedded in the language structures themselves: language used aesthetically to evoke 'an inviolable whole'. It therefore follows that appraisal based on arts talk will be holistic and qualitative rather than mechanistic or quantitative. The advantage we see in the use of conversational talk to explore and elicit aesthetic understanding is that it furnishes the appraisers (both teacher and pupil) with relevant, subjective, yet public evidence upon which to base reasoned judgements.

In the case studies that follow we attempt to reflect the synthesis of language and content and our analysis is offered in a descriptive and discursive form. The more analysis we have undertaken the more we have come to understand the data and the operations identified in our process model of the arts curriculum. The process model has helped us to interrogate and evaluate the conversations; but these living encounters have, in turn, elucidated the model, rendering our understanding of it more subtle and fluid, while seeming to confirm its basic structure.

4

CASE STUDIES

Introduction

During the course of the field work we collected a substantial amount of pupil–teacher conversational talk, recorded on video and audio tape (see Table 2).

As has already been made clear, the character and purpose of the talk was increasingly subject to guidance from the project as the different phases succeeded each other and as we continued to experience difficulty in eliciting the particular kind of talk we were interested in. Brief examples have already been cited, including one conversation from phase 3 which in many respects satisfied our criteria (pp. 42–5). The case studies that follow have been chosen for detailed analysis and interpretation which will, we feel, be useful in facilitating discussion and apprehension of the project's central concerns. Our hope is that our readers, by working through the material presented here, will be encouraged to engage directly with the problems that we have been grappling with and be impelled to draw their own conclusions and perhaps to adapt the lessons and insights to their personal needs and practices. Given the constraints within which we had to work, we hope allowance will be made

Table 2 Breakdown of the pupil–teacher conversations

| | No. of teachers and conversations | | | | | | | | |
| | Phases 1, 2 and 3 schools | | | | Phase 4 schools | | | | |
Subject	A	B	C	D	E	F	G	H	Total
Art									
Teachers	–	–	1	1	1	1	–	1	5
Conversations	–	–	5i, 1g	4i	2i	1i	–	2i	14i, 1g
Music									
Teachers	–	1	2	2	1	–	–	1	7
Conversations	–	1g	9i	2i, 4g	2i	–	–	2i	15i, 5g
Drama									
Teachers	1	1	2	1	1	–	1	1	8
Conversations	6i	1g	6i	3i, 2g	2i	–	2i	2i	21i, 3g
Dance									
Teachers	–	–	–	–	–	1	–	–	1
Conversations	–	–	–	–	–	1i, 1g	–	–	1i, 1g
English									
Teachers	–	–	2	2	–	–	–	–	4
Conversations	–	–	6i, 1g	4i, 1g	–	–	–	–	10i, 2g

i, Conversations with an individual pupil. g, Conversations with a group of two or more pupils.
Total numbers involved were: schools, 8; teachers, 25; individual pupils, 70; groups of pupils, 12; conversations, 82.

for the skew of the sample – no claim is advanced that we have achieved balanced or adequate cover of the different arts subjects or of school populations and environments. Four of the case studies (numbers 1–4) are pupil–teacher conversations – each supplies some evidence of what we were looking for. Fictional names have been used in these particular studies to protect the anonymity of the participants. The remaining three studies (numbers 5–7) are experimental conversations undertaken by the project, in an attempt to generate evidence, through talk, of aesthetic understanding at work and to learn more about the language and dynamics of such conversations. They are not intended to be seen as models of exemplary conversations. Indeed one of them, case study 6, is included precisely because its inherent shortcomings gave rise to a number of important lessons for us and helped us to draw out fresh insights about the publication mode. In case studies 5 and 7 we adopt a number of 'projective' strategies for eliciting and exploring sensate constructs. We feel that much more work needs to be done to extend and evaluate such procedures, before they can become a legitimate feature of the assessment conversation.

These additional studies stretch the research construct beyond our initial brief and reveal more of its range and potential as an assessment instrument. Of the 80 conversations recorded, disappointingly few could sustain the kind of analysis of transformation we have proposed.

We have been in pursuit of an idea. We believe that the case studies have brought us closer to understanding what has, for much of the time, been no more than guesswork. We realize that the idea, in so far as we have been able to identify and present it, now remains to be translated into a systematic assessment practice and tested for its serviceability and usefulness.

Our analysis and interpretation of the case studies seek to illuminate the following issues and ideas:

1 Our notion of aesthetic understanding – that particular process of perception or apprehension that finds meaning and significance in the contemplation and production of sensuous forms. In the course of this book we have used a number of different words in an effort to catch the range of nuances attaching to this central concept, e.g. percipience, apperception, intelligent feeling, cognitive feeling. Each of these studies shows

evidence of aesthetic understanding at work. In some instances the evidence is meagre, usually because the talk fails either to elicit it or support it more fully. In other cases the evidence is rich and intricate.

2 The four transitional operations of our process model: conventionalization (aspects of authenticity and ownership; disinterested interest in the work now let into the public domain of culture and convention where reasoned validation occurs in reflection); appropriation (of skills, knowledge and understanding from the cultural stock in the presence of impulse, of personal feelings seeking expression); transformation (the reciprocal interaction of feeling and form, i.e. as cognitive feeling; the identification of surface and depth constructs in artworks as the embodiment of understanding); publication (the expression and communication of feeling for praise by publics both familiar and unfamiliar, including creative talk about specific art work).

3 The nature of 'conversational talk' – its characteristic content and structure, its positive ambience and reflective tempo, its inherent inconclusiveness, the importance of praise and playfulness, its dynamic creativity, its presentness, its imaginativeness, and finally its clarity and reasonableness.

4 The social relationship between the conversants – supportive, reciprocal, non-judgemental, convivial, mutually empowering. The negotiation of control and the validation of knowledge.

Case study 1: The Harmonious Potter

Frank and Susie

This is a conversation between a secondary school art teacher (Frank) and a ninth-year pupil (Susie) about a small clay sculpture depicting a group of three musicians performing together.

We quote the conversation in full as an example of how the range and boundaries of a particular art teacher's aesthetic judgements (or more precisely, of the boundaries he considers appropriate to the artistic experience of a 13-year-old pupil) can determine the scope and direction of the encounter. Interviewed after the conversation Frank expressed the belief that

The Harmonious Potter

when children are dealing with a material that they find it's usually not that easy to handle and they have to concentrate on the practical side, the more unconscious, imaginative, creative side tends to take a back seat for them.

He also confessed himself surprised at the high quality of the responses the pupil was able to give.

> I was a bit surprised when she answered as well as she did, because I've never spoken to her that much before. [He had been teaching her for three years.]

Many of Frank's questions are concerned with the successful execution of skills (conventionalization). These are his basic criteria for aesthetic merit: they determine for him what looks and is good. Susie is to a great extent constrained by the context of the talk to frame responses that accord with the teacher's agenda. Occasionally, however, her turns suggest a willingness to offer alternative interpretations and ways of valuing – possibilities that go largely unrealized.

The conversation is broken down into extracts in order to make our commentary more manageable. Together the extracts constitute a whole conversation.

> F: OK, Susie, it's a lovely piece of work here. How did you first start it? What started you off?
>
> S: Well, first we watched a video of how an artist followed the movements of a ballet dancer and then sketched it down on to paper, just in black ink, and   5 make the movements show. And no expression or anything, just the movements.
>
> F: Yes, it was the movements that were most important about the exercise, was it?
>
> S: Yes.   10
>
> F: Yeah. OK, so where did the movement of the ballet dancers, then, get you to move towards musicians? These drawings [indicates sketches] presumably came somewhere in between?
>
> S: Yeah, people started modelling in class for us. Quick   15 draws – we were only allowed so much time to do them. And then we picked one of our favourite drawings – the ones we thought we'd do best – and put them into clay or other kind of material.
>
> F: What other material? Did you have a choice?   20
>
> S: Yeah, we could use wire, we could use the papier mâché and things like that.

F: So why did you choose clay?

S: Well, I find it easier to work with clay and I like being
able to make people look real, I like giving expressions. 25

F: Yes, and you find you can get more detail in clay?

S: Yes.

F: Yes, well, you've certainly got that. Very nice. [Pause.]

The first extract (1–28) follows a fairly predictable pattern, where
Frank asks Susie to rehearse the making process. To a large extent
this is simply an exercise in recall – a result, partly at least, of the
contrived research situation, but also indicative of Frank's instinct
to check that Susie has understood the instructions and executed
the task correctly. It should be noted that talk which concentrates
largely on process generates few sensate constructs in relation to the
art work, since the art work itself is not the real focus of attention.

At line 26 Frank supplies an answer to his own question by
reinterpreting what Susie has said: her 'giving expressions' becomes
his 'get[ting] more detail'. She complies with this and he commends
her on the way she has succeeded in meeting his criteria. The conversation progresses according to Frank's existing constructs at the
expense of exploring Susie's preferences. How might he have
avoided this?

A few suggestions   It might have been possible to talk imaginatively about *what* Susie had made: the 'what' of the piece, rather
than the 'how'. How evocative is the image for her? If the
people are 'real' (her term, line 25), who are they, what is their
relation to one another? Beyond that, do these things matter? To
whom? Clay allows Susie to get more detail, to give 'expressions',
but what expressions has she given? What are her figures express-
ing? Questions such as these would encourage *the active participa-*
tion of the pupil in a new act of looking and engagement. They are
questions that require subjective answers; technical considerations
would not be sufficient and neither would summative evaluations be
appropriate at this stage. Additionally and crucially they are questions that might be asked in a genuine spirit of enquiry, since the
enquirer could not presume to know better or know the right
answers already. In such a mode Frank is divested of privileged
authority. Static fact becomes fluid fiction: the risks are greater
and the normal rules that give control to the teacher and precedence
to his or her opinions are broken down.

On the positive side Frank here firmly acknowledges the importance of praise – but as yet the praise lacks substance and appears
to be no more than a polite gesture.

F: Yes, well, you've certainly got that. Very nice. [Pause.]
   Um. What made you choose musicians, as opposed . . .?
   You did do drawings of other things, you said. There   30
   are one or two [points to drawings], there are
   people there.
S: Yes, people sitting on chairs and things like that.
F: And someone playing a lute.
S: Yes.   35
F: What else? Did you see more people posing in different
   positions? Or did you do more drawings than that?
S: A couple more drawings, yeah. There were two boys,
   wrestling with each other. But I thought that would be
   quite difficult to put into clay, because it's quite   40
   complicated, getting the arms and things in the right place.
   And musicians? Well I'm interested in music and I thought
   some of my drawings and sketches were quite good of
   musicians, and good things to go off to start making
   the clay.   45
F: So in fact your knowledge of musical instruments
   helped you with the positioning of the hands of the
   flautist and of somebody playing the guitar or the lute
   there?
S: Yes.   50
F: What about the bass player, did you have a bass player
   to look at?
S: No, I didn't, um, I started off with the flute and the guitar
   and then I decided to put another one in. I took a photo
   from off a magazine and modelled it off that, so I could   55
   have an all round view of everything, so I could . . .
F: Have an all round . . .
S: So it would look interesting all the way round.
F: Oh, I see. So the viewer can look from here and there
   [turns it, gesturing the different perspectives]. It does 60
   look very nice. Good. [Pause.] It's not been glazed.
   You've only recently finished this?

Frank continues to investigate the processes of sketching and selecting that contributed to the production of the piece. Susie demonstrates that she explored various possibilities and (38–45) considered potential technical difficulties. When she mentions musicians she indicates a personal interest in the content of her piece which goes beyond the consideration of its technical feasibility. Frank's response (46–49) to this revelation of personal inclination is merely to note its functional relevance. He misses an opportunity to investigate the meaning of the piece (its surface and depth counters).

At lines 53–56 and 58 Susie introduces a new idea. She wanted to have three rather than two musicians in order to change the compositional effect of the piece. She has abandoned the life sketches in order to satisfy the demands of the evolving piece. Frank responds to her explanation, understanding and commending it but not pursuing its implications. There is no development of *how* the piece looks nice from the different perspectives it invites; instead attention is turned to the glaze. (Susie returns to her idea of constructing perspectives later on.) Frank exerts a strong pull away from transformation and appropriation and back to conventionalization.

F: Oh, I see. So the viewer can look from here and there
[turns it, gesturing the different perspectives]. It does   60
look very nice. Good. [Pause.] It's not been glazed.
You've only recently finished this?
S: Yes, it's only just been . . .
F: Was there no time to glaze it? [Touches it.]
S: No.   65
F: Would you like to glaze it?
S: Yes, I think it makes a nice finish on it.
F: It has a unity at the moment, though, we can see it all
together [circular gesture] because there are no
separate colours, but how would you – would you put   70
different colours on there or would you . . . ?
S: [thoughtful] I don't know.
F: . . . glaze it with just one glaze?
S: I might do two different colours, to get . . . I don't know
really [quiet, moves hand a little as if to touch it, but   75
stops]. I haven't really thought about it . . . [hesitant].
F: How do you think you would go about it if you did?

[S shifts around in her seat, looks uncomfortable.] If
you're not sure about putting colour on what might you
do now at this stage? [Pause, she stares at it, non-   80
plussed, turns to him and gives him a friendly smile.]
Might you try it or perhaps do some designs or
drawings or try some little wash pictures? [Mimes brush
strokes, she looks back at model.]

S: Yeah, probably, yeah.   85
F: [remembers] I think that in the film we saw, the woman
   was . . .
S: Yeah, just putting a couple of colours on . . .
F: . . . doing that. I don't know whether you could do it
   on sculpture.   90
S: No.
F: It may not look so good on sculpture, but it's something
   to think about.
S: Yes.

This extract is largely unfruitful in deepening or expanding Susie's
apperception of the work. Asked to think of how she might progress
with the piece, the pupil is uncertain; she hasn't yet given it much
thought and in this context where the piece is physically out of her
control, she doesn't seem able to think. Frank's suggestions at lines
77–84 seem arbitrary, too hypothetical, merely concerned with
technique or convention and rule rather than impulse. Susie's smile
perhaps betrays a sympathetic recognition of this. Again Frank
seems to be seeking evidence of technical mastery.

His comment (68–71) on the unity of the piece is interesting,
however. It sets up an opposition (unperceived) with the idea
(unexplored) of different perspectives: 'We can see it all together'
but we can also see it 'from here and there'. The interplay of
togetherness and separation starts to develop as an important
sensate construct in the conversation.

F: Do you think you've achieved the movement that you   95
   originally intended, because that was one of the main
   aims, wasn't it? How successful have you been in your
   aim?
S: I think I did quite well, because I got the arms in the right
   position or tried to. And I got the fingers in the right   100

places for the instruments. And I got them holding the
instruments and got how they stood and sat and things
like that.

F: But does that itself give it movement? Just because
they're holding it in the right way does that itself give   105
the sculpture movement? Or is it the way you've related
one shape to another that creates movement?

S: Well, I think it's relating one shape to another, because
it makes it more whole and sort of as if they're all
playing together and, like, making music. [Eyes light up,   110
smiles.]

F: Yes, it does. [Brief surprised look.]

S: [simultaneously] So it's a lot of things.

F: ['Links' the different figures with a rhythmical gesture of
his hand.] How aware were you of relating one shape to   115
another? The guitarist, for instance, leads on to the bass
player's arm, which takes you round to the top of the
bass and around the arm of this player. The arm of the
flautist here seems to link here. How well aware of that
were you? Were you aware of it when you made it or   120
not?

S: Well, not really, I think I just, they came all together
kind of. You know I put them back to back so that it
would all follow round, but I wasn't really aware that
all the arms were joining with each other. [Hands   125
move close to her own body in sympathy with the
sculpture.]

F: Do you think it was luck? Or did you try moving them in
slightly different positions? [Gestures around model.]
Did you perhaps try the lute player around here   130
[pointing] and the bass player there? Did you do a
little drawing of it?

S: No, I tried different positions but I thought the lute player
would look best in the front because it was the smallest
and you could see the two behind her [points, close to   135
her, looks up at Frank] playing as well, behind. I thought
it would be a nice front feature and you could see the
other two on the sides as well [points] instead of having
her behind, or something like that. And most people sit
down to play the guitar or the lute, so, I thought it   140

would be good to have them like that and sort of beginning
to the sculpture and then going round the back.
F: Um. Good [very softly]. [Pause.]

At lines 95–98 Frank asks Susie to appraise her piece with regard
to the aim for the project. He speaks of 'her' aim, however. The
consideration of how movement is conveyed by static form is
introduced and given legitimacy within the school context – the
task as set by Frank.

Susie gives a positive evaluation of her achievement, substantiating it with attention to the detail of the piece (99–103). Frank
helpfully prompts her towards the technical notion of the related-
ness of the parts as creating 'movement' in a static object. His
challenging suggestion is readily accepted by Susie who clinches the
idea of 'wholeness' and immediately arrives at a new perception
that the physical relation between the players is somehow also a
'musical' (a depth) relation. The progression of her thought can
almost be traced as she looks and speaks (108–110): 'I think it's
relating one shape to another, because it makes it more whole and
sort of as if they're all playing together and, like, making music.'
The imaginative leap shows on her face and in her eyes. The
transformation which takes place can be more clearly understood
if represented as a cluster of related constructs, where each suc-
cessive one signifies a shift from surface to depth, from physical to
symbolic meaning:

related	—	separate
whole	—	parts
all playing together	—	(disjointed)
making music	—	not making music
		(making sculpture?)

The movement from surface to depth constitutes a synthesis of
disparate sensations – of sight and sound. She has discovered symbolic resonance between the tangible sculpture and the intangible
harmonies of music and music making.

Frank, however, does little more than briefly acknowledge Susie's
insight. He returns to his investigation of the process and evaluation of her achievement in terms of the task set, monitoring her
awareness of the technical qualities of the piece. It is notable that
while he (115–121) is able to offer a sensitive guide to the aesthetic,

structural continuity he perceives within the piece, he needs to couch this in such a way as to interrogate Susie's knowledge of art process and convention. He develops this in lines 128–132, deflecting attention from the way the piece *now* works, what Susie can now perceive, to a consideration of luck, intention and process. Again he wants to discover how much she has appropriated in the *practical* mode. He has no real sense of *her* agenda (and she does have one).

In effect Frank continues to require Susie to respond to his agenda, his teacherly way of regarding the object, but fails to respond in turn. In his follow-up interview he indicated a belief that areas outside his agenda were also probably beyond Susie's abilities. Yet it is Susie who seems here to initiate a movement to *another way of looking*. If Frank were able to recognize Susie's flexibility and resource in adapting to *his* questions, *his* agenda, *his* tasks, he would better appreciate her potential for exploring other areas. At the moment he gives her credit only for the tasks – mental and physical – that he controls. He 'sees' her work but not as she sees it.

At lines 133–142 Susie expands on her earlier ideas about the composition of the piece, showing a careful consideration of how each individual element relates to the whole. She has a notion of the piece having a front and a beginning which then continues round. She seems to have in mind a very particular sequence of looking. Frank accepts and praises her account without apparently finding in it any room for expansion.

F: Um. Good [very softly]. [Pause.] And now, what, how do you feel about the thing altogether now [circular   145 gesture towards it], now that you've finished it? 'Cos you finished this about three weeks ago now – you changed groups.

S: Yes, yeah. [Leans back, shifts around.]

F: Looking at it now, because . . . have you seen it fired   150 before?

S: No.

F: You hadn't? Well I fired it more or less just after you finished it. So looking at it again, it looks like a new thing, does it? [Smiles at her.]   155

S: Yeah. [Smiles, nods, looking at it.]

F: Does it? It looks quite fresh to you? It does when I do

my work. I look at it a few weeks later [*S* looks across
at him] and it looks quite different. So how do you feel
about it now? 160

S: Well, I think it turned out quite well, how they all join
together – not sort of all separated off from one another.
It looks like they're in a group [gesturing towards it].
And how they're holding the instruments and things
like that, and how they're all standing or sitting and 165
. . . I've got different levels in it. I think I did quite
well. It's one of my best pieces of clay work I think.
[Looking up at him.]

F: Uhm. I think so. And it's surprising isn't it too [leans
forward to turn it] that, um, musicians don't actually 170
touch usually when they're playing.

S: No. [Shakes head.]

F: And yet you've had to make these touch . . .

S: Yeah. [Nods head.]

F: . . . to make this a practical piece of sculpture. And, 175
er, you're not too aware that they're touching, are you?

S: No, there's something, I mean they're not all stuck
together, they're all separated, but their backs are
all joined together.

F But what I mean is that you're not conscious of that. 180
[Turns it.] It doesn't worry you that they're touching?

S: No, no.

F: Good, okay. Thank you, Susie.

Towards the end of the conversation, Frank finally asks Susie to
reflect on the piece as it is now (143–148). He introduces the idea
(153–155) that it is perhaps no longer familiar. Susie responds
willingly to the suggestion of newness, and registers quick surprise
when he tells her (157–160) that this is a personal experience for
him too, after the firing process. It is curious that it has taken so
long for the recognition of the piece as somehow new, to be acknowledged in the conversation. It is a reminder of how much of the
conversation has been addressed to the past (process) or to a
hypothetical future (further process). The piece has not only not
been acknowledged as new – in the narrow sense of its looking
unfamiliar after firing – it has not been looked at 'in another way'.

Asked to say how she feels about the piece (157–168), Susie gives a well formed account that summarizes the sense of compositional unity, but conveys also a sense of the variety to be found within that. She includes a brief description of what the forms actually represent, the accuracy of observation. There is consistency here. The structure of her response is interesting – beginning and ending with judgements, which in between are substantiated by an account of the piece's significant qualities (significant within the terms of this conversation: she doesn't include her 'making music' insight as a reason for judging it 'good'). This is an act of conventionalization (and it is perhaps right that Frank should put the question to her at this stage). The piece is endorsed by him, summatively.

In the final turns Frank offers a further interpretation or appreciation of the piece which appears to derive from what has already been said. His comments (169–171, 173, 175–176) are revealing of his aesthetic criteria and could be reworded as a statement that 'sculpture must be both practically feasible and close to actuality, lifelike. It should not therefore draw attention to its non-literal aspects.' Susie appears to comply with his comments but her interpretative response (177–179) suggests that she hasn't picked up on his main point, which he then reformulates. By implication, a consciousness of the musicians touching would be a source of worry. It is by no means clear that this would be Susie's own response, though she is not in a position to query his assumption. Her public valuing is dependent upon his criteria of what counts in sculpture in school.

This conversation is an illuminating example of a teacher getting so much right, yet ultimately seeming to miss the point. He begins by praising her and quickly gets her looking at the piece. They explore its content and the process of production. He helps her to become conscious of her own achievement in creating a sense of movement in the piece, and in giving it formal coherence. On the video tape his gentle, concerned and considerate manner are thoroughly reassuring and commendable. Susie is at ease with him and he, for his part, finds her a pleasure to be with and her work surprisingly committed. In conversation with us afterwards he was regretful that the pressure of day-to-day school routine meant that, despite having taught her for three years, he felt that he hardly knew her. Indeed the conversation had been a unique opportunity to contact her – it reminded him that a whole dimension of his life as a teacher seemed to be missing.

From our point of view, however, Frank fails to connect with

Susie's motives, or with the imaginative and expressive dimensions embodied in the sculpture and latent in the conversation. Susie is left only with a somewhat teacherly endorsement of her success in carrying through the task as set. The momentary flickers and gleams of mutual feeling and percipience quickly die away as Frank reverts to his own agenda and deploys his own criteria. His praise therefore cannot work for Susie to validate her feelings and perceptions. In terms of our process model, Frank operates largely from the position of and in terms of quadrant 1. No potential space is opened up for mutual play. He obtains no insight into her impulse or into the imaginative process by which she sought to make clay sound.

Case study 2: Marching Orders

Michael and Fiona

Here again we have a secondary art teacher (Michael) and an eleventh-year pupil (Fiona) talking about a piece of sculpture. If anything, in this next discussion, the teacher opts for an even more teacherly role, quickly establishing the game as a kind of treasure hunt: he has something on his mind and she has to try and guess what it is. Once again the opportunities for a living, *present* exploration of the sensate qualities of the work are there, but are sacrificed to a rigid, prepared programme more reminiscent of an MoT test than a personal conversation. The teacher allows for neither spontaneity nor play. Arts assessment is here conceived as a kind of vocabulary test.

The following discussion is taken from the third phase of the project, where we had worked out a seven-point 'agenda' which we felt would enable participants to cover all areas of possible aesthetic interest. We did not intend the points to be inhibiting to the free and meandering nature of conversation but rather to offer ways or categories by which a teacher or pupil might retrospectively make sense of the discoveries made through talk. Unfortunately, Michael insisted on using the agenda as a checklist. (The agenda is given in Chapter 2.)

The subject of the conversation is a clay head, positioned on a display/decorating wheel that Michael occasionally turns. Fiona does not either touch the head at any point or give a turn to the wheel.

Marching Orders

The first extract occurs early in the conversation after Fiona has described the head as 'fighting' and 'grotesque' – it appears to represent a yelling sergeant-major. Michael supplies the word 'aggressive' to synthesize Fiona's terms and here proposes that they explore the notion of 'aggressive form'.

M: Is there something in that form? If it were an abstract
thing, do you think you could make an abstract
sculpture which had the properties in this to make it
an aggressive sculpture without it being an army
officer's face? Do you think it's possible to do that?   5
F: I think so. The thing that makes it aggressive is its
face – it looks so shocked and angry. If you made it
really bold, really . . . lines or bold pieces of clay, not
just fiddly, make it really bold and strong.
M: Yeah. So you could in a way. I mean there are forms   10
. . . I mean, what did that picture – sorry, this head –
what makes it aggressive? Do you know what forms
there are that make it aggressive?
F: Um. No, not really.
M: No? Have a little think about it. Have another look at it.   15

In lines 1–5 Michael asks Fiona to consider the form of the
actual head in opposition to a hypothetical 'abstract' form and to
identify common properties which might make it possible for both
to be described as aggressive. He is challenging her to distinguish
'universal' expressive forms from a particular narrative content (the
soldier character). The idea is, in itself, interesting and complex.
Fiona responds (6–9) by referring first to the actual head then to
Michael's hypothetical abstract form. From 'shocked' and 'angry' she
derives 'bold', 'not fiddly', 'strong', appropriately transforming
representational qualities into sensate constructs.

The extract is interesting because it shows the way in which sensate
constructs can be generated in the particular. Fiona is allowed to do
this to a certain extent (6–9), but the framework on which Michael
asks her to build is not sufficiently grounded in the surface aspects of
the piece. This means that though she can abstract away from the
piece – can think of potential material forms which might signify
'shocked' and 'angry' – she cannot (14) reverse the process when
asked to consider *actual* form. 'Shocked' and 'angry' are 'depth'
counters which have not been apprehended at the surface level of
the piece. This suggests a failure on the part of Michael to understand
the making of constructs, the processes of aesthetic engagement.

What seems unfortunate is the way in which Michael's questions
require the pupil to respond in a hypothetical mode. This is simply
a mistaken strategy. The talk moves away from the particular object

of attention in the search for a generalizable answer to be culled
somehow from a repertoire of art knowledge and returns to the piece
only once a construct has been established that says there are
generalized and recognizable 'aggressive' forms.

Fiona is asked to talk hypothetically about abstract art, which
her piece is not, and to abstract from that piece 'properties' of
aggressiveness. In this process the properties lose their relation to the
piece itself. The forms 'that make it aggressive' are related neither to
Fiona's personal perception nor to the individuality of the image, but
to general categories, public knowledge, cultural norms (as mediated
by Michael). *It is as if the head were not there and as if Fiona had
not made it.* At line 15, asking her to look again at the head, Michael
asks her to find what he, in a sense, has found and named. Eventually
he takes her through his interpretation of the piece and prompts
her into a recognition of its 'aggressive forms'.

M: There are things in that head which are to do with
   aggressive forms. Do you know what they are?
F: Um. No, I . . .
M: What about the eyes, for example?
F: They look shocked, they . . .   20
M: Uhm. what makes them look shocked?
F: The way the eyebrows and the eyes are quite far
   apart and he's looking down, and they're quite wide
   as well.
M: Uhm. So, wide. They're [mimics the expression],   25
   aren't they? What about the nostrils?
F: They're flaring [smiles].
M: Flaring nostrils now. The mouth?
F: That's just open as if he's going to exclaim something.
M: So he's exclaiming, he's shouting [affirming tone,   30
   satisfaction]. And nostrils . . . flaring. Like a poem, isn't
   it? I mean, what . . . so why are his nostrils flaring?
   What actually would create that? Think about it.
   What's a nostril doing if it's flaring? What actually
   would create that? Is it just being aggressive or is it   35
   [breathes in heavily] breathing? It's breathing in, isn't
   it? Taking in more oxygen, because of the force he's
   going to have to give out.
F: Yeah [whisper].

In this extract, the representational/depictive/natural elements of the piece – eyes, brows, nostrils, mouth – are assessed as confirmatory instances of the dominant character of the piece – aggressive form – which has been supplied by the teacher. Their significance, the way they signify, is elicited so as to match the existing category. Their signifying potential suffers a reduction. (All this is characteristic of non-aesthetic looking.) As a result, the eyes, for instance, seem shocked in a general rather than particular way – they become substitutions in a formula. Michael appears to be inviting Fiona to think in stereotypes.

On the basis of this extract it is not possible to comment on Fiona's aesthetic response at all. Although it is she who offers descriptors for the elements of the head, she does so under Michael's strict control. He acknowledges only those aspects of her response which confirm his sense of what is appropriate. His seeing legitimizes hers. At lines 22–24, for example, Fiona offers an extended account of why the eyes look shocked: 'The way the eyebrows and the eyes are quite far apart and he's looking down, and they're quite wide as well.' Michael is selective in what he responds to in this account: 'Uhm. So, wide . . .'. He 'sees' only that aspect of her response which confirms his existing knowledge/formulation: 'shocked eyes' equal 'wide eyes'. (We can infer from this that he sees less in the piece than she does.) It is noticeable that the part of Fiona's account that is ignored by Michael contains some carefully observed detail of the compositional structure of the face: the brows are 'up' while the gaze is down, and the wideness seems to be in the relation of these two elements as well as in the eyes as discrete entities.

At line 29 Fiona elaborates on her description: the mouth is not simply 'open', but 'open *as if* ' – she begins to assign depth meaning to the piece – to connect form with feeling, with imagination, in terms of some particular exclamation. Michael might have wondered here what was about to be exclaimed but instead he assimilates her words to his meaning – 'exclaiming' as another instance of generalized aggressive form.

M: So do you feel it's ugly? Do you think it's attractive?   40
   How do you feel about it? [Turning head.]
F: I think he's . . . I think he's quite comical [smiles]. I
   laugh at it sometimes.
M: Yes, I think it's quite comical, yes.

F: [lively] When I walk into the room and see him I   45
      laugh.
M: Yes. Can you think of a word to describe that? What
      might be . . . what might make it like that?
F: [Pauses, looks at him.] I can't think of a word but I think
      it's exaggerated.   50
M: [speaking quickly] Sort of like a parody, a caricature,
      isn't it? It's almost a caricature of an army officer,
      isn't it? I mean, because it's so exaggerated it
      becomes a humorous piece, doesn't it? Do you
      think it's. . . [pause]. Do you think it has any sensuality?   55
      Do you know what I mean by sensuality?
F: [Shakes head.]
M: Do you think people would want to feel it? [Puts his
      hands over it.]

At lines 40–41 Michael offers the simple descriptive construct
ugly–attractive as an invitation to the pupil to explore her aesthetic
feelings. (This construct is important to him because he wants to
raise the idea of attractive ugliness – he does this later when he
introduces the example of Francis Bacon.) Fiona is not confined by
his construct, but supplies an idea of her own. She conveys (42–43,
45–46) how alive and personal her sense of the comedy is. She refers
to the head quite spontaneously as 'he' – in contrast to Michael's 'it'.
While Fiona's anecdotal 'When I walk into the room and see him I
laugh' helps to free the conversation, Michael's response has the
opposite effect. His request for a 'word' to describe her spontaneous
response suggests a desire to elicit concrete and citable evidence of
an 'appropriate' kind. She is being quizzed here. There can be very
few other contexts beside the school room in which a comment such
as 'When I walk into the room and see him I laugh' would be
responded to with the question 'Can you think of a word to describe
that?' Fiona seems to understand that Michael requires a correct
answer and closure, but can only convey her sense that the sculpture
is 'exaggerated'. Michael picks up on this word and interprets it,
synthesizing her sense of exaggeration and humour into the notion
of parody or caricature – another category-term to be acquired.
Having achieved this the topic is closed and a new agenda item –
sensuality – is introduced, abruptly. (He is working through his
checklist.)

The idea of parody or caricature brings with it possible considerations of realism, portraiture (if this is a caricature, who or what is the reality?), the selection and composition of features. None of these possibilities is explored here. The idea is rushed over, allowing no opportunity for Fiona to respond. Again it is as if the destination has been reached with no journey having been undertaken. (As a caricature the head has little substance. It has neither surface nor depth counters.)

Michael opens the discussion to a consideration of surface qualities (sensuality), but he does so in such a way as to present them as a separate issue. If the activity of aesthetic response is a searching for connectedness, Michael's approach does not seem to allow for it. Sensation, sensuality, supervenes over meaning and, in any event, is itself left unexplored.

M: Do you feel satisfied with your work? 60
F: Yeah.
M: How do you feel satisfied about it?
F: I like how it's turned out – it's how I wanted it to look.
   I wanted it to look like this. I wanted it to look old
   and angry and sort of like [M turns head towards him] 65
   his own, sort of like not perfect [gestures]. I mean, his
   head's very rough, he's very dipped, he's got lots of
   dips, he's like chiselled or something. And then the
   ears aren't perfect ears and the nose isn't right but it
   looks good to me. I think it's turned out very nice. 70
M: Uhm. Great. And, er, [remembering] you had a
   problem with it, didn't you?
F: Yeah it blew up in the kiln and when I took it off the
   head stand it completely collapsed, but I fixed his
   face back. 75
M: Yeah, you didn't quite get it as symmetrical as it was,
   did you?
F: No, but I think it's better than the way it was.
M: Yeah. You think it's better? [Turning it round.]
F: Yeah. 80
M: Do you?
F: Yeah, I made it with sort of angles the same [hands
   up, gesturing].
M: [interjects] Symmetrical before, was it?

F: Yeah.   85
M: But now you like that asymmetry?
F: Yeah.
M: This side's coming out more than that side, isn't it?
F: Didn't want his face to fall off, but since it did I made
   the best of it.   90
M: [moving head around] So what's it . . . Ah! So what
   do you feel it does then, that asymmetry? Why do you
   prefer the asymmetry?
F: Because people themselves aren't symmetrical – their
   left and right aren't exact and his isn't either. But   95
   [whispers] I hate really perfect, completely perfect
   things.
M: Uhm. So this is a bit more imperfect?
F: Yeah.

In this extract the Fiona's particular and personal engagement
with the work begins to be uncovered. By pursuing his first question
at line 62, Michael prompts Fiona to 'publicize' her feelings for
and perceptions of the piece (63–70). The dynamic of her explica-
tion is interesting. She first makes a positive judgement of the
work, relating the outcome to what she desired. She then substan-
tiates the judgement with sensate evidence found within the piece.
This is at both depth and surface levels. In effect she identifies
feelings ('old', 'angry') with form ('rough', 'dipped', 'chiselled').
She creates a complex depth construct which fuses imperfection
with goodness. Finally she reiterates her judgement, which is now
based upon an argued case for subjective 'rightness' (as opposed to
objective or technical rightness). There is crucial evidence of transformation here in her attention to sensate form and the way in which
it expresses. Her belief in the validity of her own judgement ('it
looks good to me') strongly indicates that she has moved past the
appropriation stage and has come full circle to a point where her
feelings are experienced as legitimate within the larger cultural
context: she has re-entered conventionalization.

Further support for this emerges in the following turns where they
recall a hitch in the making process that spoiled the symmetry of
the original head. At lines 73–75 and 78 Fiona expresses her conviction that this was fortuitous but fortunate. She shows again that it
is meaningful perception of the head as it is now that underlies her

positive judgement rather than an adherence to successful technical design and execution. She clearly asserts her ownership but is at the same time 'disinterested' – the piece is now *public*; it is independent of her making.

Michael appears pleased with both Fiona's account (63–70) and her liking for its asymmetry. He is distracted, however, by ensuring that she knows and uses the correct vocabulary, and by a desire (91–93) to generalize, to move into general statements. Fiona reiterates (94–97) her complex sense of the rightness of formal imperfection.

In the kind of talk we are looking for the adult should be prepared to offer a good deal of his or her responses to the work under scrutiny – but only when the child has had time to find her own responsive ground under her feet. Then the adult's additional material works to enrich and fine-tune the pupil–artist's own perceptions. Here, Michael firmly imposes his reading upon the art work from the outset and, on the basis of what *he* sees, sets Fiona a kind of obstacle course in order to test and control her responses. Her incipient playfulness – readiness to have an actual conversation and to engage directly with her image as present to her there and then – is consistently resisted and subverted by Michael, who may, perhaps, have responded rather too dutifully to our instructions and governed his own behaviour accordingly, despite our insistence that the project agenda should not be made to function as a checklist. This uncomfortable discussion shows what can happen when the teacher is unable or unwilling to meet the pupil on the ground of her own sensing.

Case study 3: Catching Words

Ben and Kenny

This conversation takes place during an actual class lesson, between a tenth-year pupil (Kenny) and his English teacher (Ben). Ben's expectations of Kenny's 'speaking' ability were not high, and he was impressed and surprised by the way in which Kenny was able to 'analyse' what he'd done. Ben had selected Kenny as 'a bit below average' and asked him to talk about one of his poems as a way of testing the project's approach.

Reflecting subsequently on a transcript of the conversation, Ben was critical of some of the questions he had asked and the amount of time he had allowed himself. He wondered: 'Perhaps I had too firm an idea of what *I* wanted from the conversation rather than what *he* wanted', but concluded

> I think the conversation was meaningful and we both discovered things which helped the learning process. As an unprepared conversation within a 'real' classroom I don't think such a dialogue could be any better than this.

The stimulus material for Kenny's poem was another poem written (supposedly) by a young boy about his sister who had died in hospital at only three days old. The class had been asked to write a poem based upon what the dead sister might have said to her brother. Much of the Ben–Kenny conversation is concerned with the drafting and redrafting process – an important facet of National Curriculum English – which means that there is little direct attention to the formal elements of the poem or to its sensuous qualities, from which surface and depth constructs would derive. Kenny is first invited to read out his finished poem.

K: 'I'm sorry, my big brother, but I still love you.
You shouldn't be crying for me but I should be crying
for you.
When you put me in your arms your hands were soft,
so soft,   5
And when you kissed me with your lips I knew our love
would last forever.
But when you put me down again I thought it would be
forever,
But when you turned and smiled at me I knew our love 10
would grow forever.'

B: How do you feel about that now, reading that now,
because that was a long time ago you wrote that?

K: It's all right. I'm not sure if I could alter it. But I like it
as it is.   15

B: Because you did quite a few draft copies of that before
you settled for that one, didn't you? So which was
your first attempt?

K: That one. [Selects another version.]

B: Right, read that.   20

K: 'I'm sorry, my big brother, but I still love you.
    You shouldn't be crying for me but I should be crying for
    you. When you put me in your arms your hands were
    soft, so soft,
    When you kissed me with your lips I knew our love   25
    would last forever.
    When you put me down again the world went so black,
    But then you came and smiled at me I knew our love
    would be forever.'

B: Now why did you change that, the first time after you'd   30
    written that?

K: Because I didn't think that the words were right in the
    way that I wrote it.

B: What was the background to this? How did you come
    to write this?   35

Ben's first move (12–13) is to elicit Kenny's current response to the
poem, which is not a recent piece of work. Kenny asserts his satisfaction with the poem while entertaining but rejecting the possibility of
change (i.e. of still further drafting). He does not substantiate his liking here. Ben does not seek to explore Kenny's liking by reference to
the poem 'as it is'. Rather he directs Kenny towards an uncovering of
method and process (16–18). *The poem is addressed as an object: the
final outcome of a series of draftings.* This emphasis is sustained
throughout the conversation. When Kenny has read his first draft he
is asked to explain the changes made (30–31) and is then taken still
further back. *No response is offered by Ben to the actual reading
itself.* It is noticeable in the few turns that follow how Kenny has to
be prompted into remembering Ben's stimulus material. This has, it
seems, become irrelevant to him, yet Ben finds it important to retrace
the sequential development fairly painstakingly.

Kenny's response at lines 32–33, which raises the question of
the 'rightness' of particular words, provides an opening for the close
consideration of both or either poem at the level of sensate ordering.
But this opportunity is not taken up. Kenny returns again to the
business of finding right words through the activity of drafting. He
amply demonstrates his appropriation of this method.

B: And did you come up with that straight away? When
    I said, 'OK I want you to write this,' did you?

K: Yeah, I came up with this one, then I started doing
other drafts, changing the words, and making it rhyme,
or tried to make it rhyme.   40

B: So what were you saying about . . . you imagined you
were in? How did you manage to write like that?

K: Oh, well, I thought, well, if I was the child that had died
I'd want the words to be more catching – of what the
child would say – like as he would say it normally but   45
in rhyming words.

B: So you imagined . . . Yes, well, you imagined you were
going to be the child, in reply to the brother. So you
did the first draft. How did you feel about that when
you'd done that?   50

K: Well, I didn't think the words were good enough – I
didn't think I'd got the point across.

B: Did you think the ideas were good?

K: Yeah, I thought the first draft was good. The second . . .
[Ben interrupts here.]   55

It is noticeable that Ben passes over Kenny's references to rhyme
(38–40), perhaps because, looking back at the poem itself, there is
little evidence of its use. With no close attention to the thing itself
this discrepancy remains undetected. In the discussion of poetry,
rhyme is an important formal *element*; one of the principal means
by which the form (language) can take on sensuous meaning. It is
on such issues, particularly as they are raised by Kenny, that the
conversation might have centred. Instead Ben attempts to focus
again on Kenny's 'management' of his writing (41–42).

Kenny's response (43–46) reveals a cluster of concepts which
combine in interesting ways:

myself	—	child
catching	—	not catching
normal	—	rhyming
normal rhyming	—	not normal rhyming

In their relation to the form of the poem these are all sensate
constructs operating both at surface and, in their interrelation, at
depth levels. Kenny projects himself into the position of the child
('if I was the child') and the finding of 'catching' words is the desire
not simply of the writer but of the writer-as-child: implicitly he

makes the distinction. Kenny's strong sense of the particular voice suggests the appropriation of feeling. It is reiterated again later in the conversation.

The word 'catching' suggests how words can encapsulate meaning: there is more here than a straight equivalence between the desire to say ('what the child *would* say') and the form (words) that will aptly say (catch) it; there is an indication of the *struggle* to embody feeling in form – transformation.

Again Kenny refers to rhyming words (perhaps as synonymous for him with poetry?). His fusion of 'rhyming' with 'normal' is clarification and complication of his previous mention of 'rightness' (32–33): the achievement of particular voice through poetry.

At lines 51–52 a further dimension is added: 'good enough' words get 'the point across'; they communicate, they mean in a real sense. Later we see how this idea of a message is crucial to Kenny.

Ben shifts attention (53) from the words to the ideas in the poem; he does not trace the ideas in the words as the place where Kenny has intimated they are to be found, but rather treats form and feeling separately, and therefore as separate.

B: Did you enjoy writing it?
K: Yeah.
B: The first one?
K: Yeah, the first one. It was difficult because I didn't
   have anything to go on, or what to write out, so I   60
   wrote that. Then did other copies, just changing the
   words, and came up with that one.
B: So you had an idea in your head and knew what the
   idea was, and thought it was a good one but you
   didn't think that [i.e. first draft] was really . . .   65
K: Good enough.
B: . . . good enough to capture the idea that you had in
   your head. So, right, what did you do then?
K: I looked at the words that I thought could need
   changing. And I experimented using different words.   70
B: What kind of words did you decide were the ones
   that needed changing?
K: The black one, 'Then the world went so black'.
B: Why did you think that that was a word that you might
   want to change?   75

K: Er, 'cos it's looking on the down side of life and
should be looking at, yeah, he's gone to a better
place – the baby that had died – and wants the brother
to know that he is all right and not to feel sorry for him.
B: So the first poem was too sad and you didn't want it   80
to be like that?
K: No, I wanted it to be happy.

At lines 59–62 our sense of Kenny's engagement with the work of
writing the poetry is deepened. He describes the drafting process as
it were 'from the inside', as transformative. The first draft was
difficult because there was nothing to sense, no material to engage
with. Drafting has become more than a learnt operation – it is
a personal process of 'making sense', i.e. of arriving at depth
meaning.

Kenny persists in referring to the words (the sensuous material of
the poetic form) and at lines 71–72 and 74–75 Ben finally helps
him to focus in upon them. The result is a rich explanation of his
decision to change the word 'black' (76–79). Again Kenny shows an
awareness of the speaking voice and the listener implied by the
poem's narrative – and implicitly of his own relation to these as the
maker of the piece. These relations remain implicit and are not
recognized by Ben. Kenny draws upon the connotative meanings
of black – it signifies 'the down side of life', an idea of finality and
nothingness in contrast to faith in 'a better place'. The single word
'black' embodies an attitude of pessimism, and as such defeats the
poet's optimistic purpose: its 'all right and not to feel sorry'. Kenny
is able to paraphrase and abstract this message from the form of his
poem. What is needed now is a return to its surface, to a deeper
investigation of whether and how these feelings find their poetic
form.

Ben, however, continues to be interested in the overall drafting
process; he summarizes the first draft as 'too sad'. Compare his
understanding of the process, which tends to treat each draft as a
single, finite entity, with that of Kenny, for whom drafting is a
moving about among words, precise attention to detail, part of
a single imaginative projection.

B: All right. And at what stage did you decide this is the
one I'm going to finish with? Why did you decide
then that you were happy with it? What was the   85

> difference between, say, the third version and the
> final one?
>
> K: With that one, everything was OK, but not good
>   enough. So I read it and just changed a few other
>   words. Then wrote it down as I thought I would say it,   90
>   so that was OK.
>
> B: When you say you read it, did you read it out loud or
>   just look at it?
>
> K: Yeah, I read it quietly in class, not in my mind itself. I
>   knew how I would say it, 'cos normally I make   95
>   mistakes if I say it in my mind.
>
> B: So you tried to put yourself in the position of being
>   the person who was speaking? You tried to imagine
>   this was you?
>
> K: Uhm.   100

Where Ben (92–93) wants to clarify (rather than accept and move on from) Kenny's explanation he achieves a valuable insight into the way Kenny goes about his sensate ordering. More often than not this is the case: that attention to and genuine enquiry into the child's meaning – expansion rather than closure – are the means by which the conversation comes to life. Here Kenny reveals through his personal practice an appreciation of sound quality as a criterion for rightness: the words do not simply mean on the page, they mean as vocalized sound. Once again Ben fails to show an interest in the sensate implications of Kenny's statement. The invitation to engage afresh with the fabric of the poem itself is disregarded.

Instead the talk moves from the specific and on to other poems that Kenny has written. Ben seems to be seeking a common thread that will form the basis for a future poetry project, but while Kenny is pleased with *this* poem he dismisses the others. His reasons reinforce his commitment to the unique utterance of the dead child as he has created and expressed it.

> B: Yeah, you found it a good poem. You found writing
>   poetry quite interesting. Would you have written . . . ?
>   Did you ever write poetry before that or . . . ?
>
> K: Yeah, in other English lessons, but I didn't think they
>   were any good so I threw those away.   105
>
> B: Why weren't they any good?

K: I don't know. None of the words rhymed, or they were
just poems with no meaning. I think that's different
because it's more lifelike.

B: So you became . . .   110

K: A person writing that, a different . . . not just me, but
the baby.

B: Right, so you became a different person, and you
found that useful for trying to write – imagine yourself
as somebody different. And also there was more   115
emotion in this one than the ones you'd written about . . .

K: Yeah, a lot more feeling in this than any of the others.

B: So if it was a good poem, and I thought it was a good
poem as well, and you were going to say 'you're
good at this, let's do it some more!', what kind of   120
poems would you need to write in order to make
them good poems as well?

K: Lifelike ones. Original ones. Things that people
haven't thought about. Things that people think are
not very good, not good enough to write about. And   125
you can make them into things – like someone's died
and you can make it into a nice one. I'd like to do
things like that.

For Kenny, working in the medium changes what he is. He is
no longer simply himself but himself as other: 'A person writing
that, a different . . . *not just me*, but the baby' (111–112). Ben
draws him out on this later in the search for another poem he
might do.

B: OK, so could you write a poem about yourself?
Because in this you're imagining you were somebody   130
else?

K: No, I couldn't write about myself.

B: Why not?

K: Because I'm probably too . . . nice to myself, writing a
poem.   135

B: What do you mean by that?

K: I'd probably write the good things about me not the
bad things.

B: How about if you imagined you being described by
somebody else? What about if you imagined that your 140

Dad was writing about you? Would you be able to do
that, do you think?

K: Er, I'm not sure. Probably I could give it a go. That
would be a bit difficult to do.

Kenny gives a sense here that the ability to take a detached view is
important to the writing of a poem. Losing oneself (disinterested-
ness) involves the crucial effort of imagination which forges the
poem – he is no longer a self, he is an actor. He understands the
function of point of view in the poem, how in taking his Dad's role
he might make it possible to see himself. Ben recognizes the use that
a pupil might make of this device, but is less successful in identifying
the particular personal impulse which motivates Kenny. At line 109
Kenny introduces the idea of 'lifelike', picking it up again at lines
123–128. The idea links interestingly with the earlier notion
(76–79) of not looking at the 'down side of life'. His desire is to take
real-life situations – the commonplace – and to treat them as
significant through the act of writing about them. This is in contrast
to the type of suggestions which Ben goes on to make for further
writing: Diego Maradona knocked out of the World Cup, Nelson
Mandela released from prison. However, it is precisely the non-
newsworthy that Kenny wishes to celebrate. And it *is* a kind of
celebration – he wants to transform sorrow into consolation; to
make the 'lifelike' 'original' through a kind of act of faith. This is his
personal vision (not too strong a word), the way in which poetry
empowers him. He stresses the transformative process – 'you can
make it *into* a nice one' – and clinches it with a statement of confidence: 'I'd like to do things like that' (127–128).

The conventionalization here is very strong too: Kenny has a clear
sense of his individual purpose and the way in which he can make
poetry work to define him as a person. He goes on to reject the
writing of love poems as too common and later, asked to consider
future possibilities, comes up with a specific instance of the general
purpose he outlined before.

B: And you're going to have a go at that? And you're   145
going to try and do those the same way and try and
imagine that you're someone else, writing about
something they feel quite strongly about? What kind
of things do you think you could do?

K: Um, I'd like to write something if someone was   150

crippled or something. I'd like to write something nice
to uplift them or something, like give them confidence
that everything's not down in the world, it's not as bad
as what it seems to be.

B: Is there anything going on in the news now that you   155
could use as an idea and say, 'If I was in that situation
this is what I would want to say about it'?

K: Nothing in the news.

Kenny's suggestion repeats both the content and structure of
the baby poem – his interest is very particular and seems acutely
felt. Ben, however, seeks to move him away from this. His move
seems premature – it places more emphasis on the production of
a good range of poetic 'samples' rather than on the crucial impulse
upon which any good poem depends. Ben and Kenny are at cross-
purposes here – Ben seems implicitly to be directed by the criteria
for exam success, Kenny by a notion of himself as an empowered
and empowering writer. These are strong feelings which Kenny
has developed through his engagement with a particular task. The
conversation has not succeeded in so far as it has only barely
returned the poet to his poem, to the arrangement of words and
thoughts which must now speak for itself. Nowhere in the conversation is Kenny's eloquent purpose brought to bear on the sounds,
textures, orderings of the things he has made. There is no re-
visiting, no praise. Notions of his aesthetic understanding may
be indirectly inferred, but remain unsubstantiated by direct sensate
construal.

In the assessment conversation the teacher must be alert to the
subtleties and complexities of a pupil's utterances, which means
listening hard, being willing to challenge meaning, and becoming
skilled at recognizing ways into the transformative heart of the
pupil's arts experience. Where a teacher does not recognize and
acknowledge the quality and interest of a pupil's utterance, does not
cause it to be developed, to generate new ideas, it is not likely, given
the nature of the school context, that the pupil will herself or himself
recognize its value. Notice, for instance, how Susie (case study 1)
leaves out her inspiration about music-making from her final self-
assessment. She has come to value her making skills but not her
insights, not the sense of the work's signification that she has
achieved in, as or through publication.

Our teachers tended to use the conversation to confirm that the lesson had been learnt. They were not really looking to penetrate the unknown in the child's perception. The teachers' surprise when they discovered that their pupils could be so articulate betrayed a low expectation of talking ability as well as of aesthetic understanding. We didn't record much teacher surprise or delight over *what* pupils actually said. Most of the rich pupil utterances we pick out here elicited little comment from the teachers either in the conversation or afterwards. In the Ben–Kenny conversation, evidence of Kenny's aesthetic understanding has to be gleaned from general, unfocused comments. There is extrinsic work to be done in unpacking constructs and relating them to formal elements. Significance is compressed. In contrast, where the conversants can engage directly with the thing itself, significance is open to scrutiny in all its scarcity or abundance. It shows itself as instances.

On his own admission Ben had underestimated Kenny. It is very clear that Kenny feels closely connected to his poem despite having written it many weeks before the conversation. He takes pleasure in recollecting the feel of what he wanted to say and is clear about the struggle he had to control the medium, in catching the right words. He is confident in publication, has a clear motive to guide his writing and a strong conviction about himself as a writer (conventionalization). For whatever reason (a teacherly concern to hurry on to the next production/project?) most of the rich potential passes by, and Kenny is denied the chance of a full reacquaintance with his poem in feeling and imagination that he might have found deeply gratifying and motivating.

Case study 4: Seeing the Light

Stan and Karen

These extracts are from a conversation on the subject of a group drama presented by year 11 pupils at the end of their first term's work for an Expressive Arts GCSE. The piece was entitled 'Futures' and had two major sections, the first showing a morning street scene and the second, in contrast, a mass of figures dressed in black, moving in slow motion under a strobe light, their arms outstretched, hands clutching. The climax of the drama was achieved with a bomb falling, the figures prostrated and then the desolate sound of a baby crying.

What we can sense of the drama's mood and quality is strongly mediated by the conversational strategies used by Stan, who is serious and pragmatic throughout. As in the Frank–Susie conversation, we can infer, from his questions and handling of Karen's responses, Stan's view of his subject, of what constitutes satisfactory meaning for drama in school. Karen's body language as caught on camera is revealing. She shrugs her shoulders and grimaces a great deal, her behaviour seeming in many cases to indicate confusion as to the *purpose* of Stan's questions, as much as her possible anxiety at having her answers recorded on videotape. Stan seemed, if anything, to have over-prepared himself for what he saw as a kind of TV interview. His unease in the research situation, masked as super-confidence, had a damaging effect upon the quality of the conversation. One way and another neither of the participants probably did themselves justice.

S: What sort of message, if there was a message, would
   you take from it yourself?
K: Um . . . um. I don't know really . . . maybe . . . um [shrugs].
S: Okay. Well, if I asked you to find some words to
   describe that opening scene, the modern scene, any   5
   words that came into your head, like, for example,
   'happy', would that describe what was going on in that
   opening scene?
K: It would have described some of it.
S: Okay. Could you think of any other words that would   10
   help to describe it?
K: 'Everyday', really.
S: Right, happy, everyday [counting on fingers].
K: Um, 'poor'. Um, like we had hair spray that was
   dropped on the floor and that sort of like showed that   15
   we're ruining our atmosphere with the ozone layer.
   And um, maybe 'sad' in a way because, like the
   tramp's on the street and no one seems to care about
   him, and maybe 'hardworking', 'cos there's Sarah, she
   was a road sweeper.   20
S: So it was a bit of all sorts of things – there was evidence of
   hard work, there was evidence of . . . caring . . . or not?

[Squints at her.] Would you say it was caring?

K: Yeah there was 'cos Donna gave Mark some money.
Or I think she did, I'm not sure. 25

S: There's also some evidence of destruction, with
something like the aerosol. Would that be fair to say?

K: Yeah.

When Stan's first question fails to elicit much of a response from Karen he reformulates it with an apparently simpler request for descriptive words. The underlying assumption seems to be that words used as labels are equivalent to meanings and messages in drama in school. It is revealing how this approach to the conversation carries an understanding of the dramatic medium that is entirely consistent with it. The way one talks about art and makes meaning from it in contemplation seems to reflect the way one actually handles the medium in making. So here, for instance, Karen gives an account of the opening scene (14–20) in which simple isolated gestures or signs such as a dropped hairspray can or a neglected tramp are to be understood as instantly and unambiguously meaningful, i.e. as 'symbolic'. Stan accepts these instances as constituting evidence, as encapsulating a message that can be exactly translated through a verbal equivalent: poverty is signalled by a dropped aerosol, sadness by an uncared-for tramp, hard work by a road sweeper. Karen has appropriated this formula for making dramatic meaning, presumably from Stan himself. The signs within the piece are used to denote rather than connote feeling. Feeling in the conversation is labelled rather than explored. Each signifier, each verbal equivalent, is accepted as discrete, integrated only as 'a bit of all sorts of things' and carries no imaginative or connotative weight.

Stan gives no indication that he sees drama as signifying in anything other than this explicit, paraphrasable way. If he does, he seems unclear how to help Karen towards greater complexity of understanding or a more integrating engagement with dramatic form. The talk produces a mechanical, closed interpretation of the drama and lacks spontaneity or flux. Karen is not encouraged to feel her way into the piece or to use words genuinely to figure out and communicate what her sensing is or was. Publication here is neither active nor confident, and results in Karen's confusion and lack of animation.

S: Yeah. So there's bits of everything in that one scene.
Okay. Let's go to the second one then. Could you find 30

words like that, that would perhaps begin to describe
that second scene?

K: Oh. Um.

S: And they can just be single words like happy.

K: I don't think it was happy. It was like poverty and   35
depression and like, um, when we were going towards
the light, I felt as if there was something there [more
animated] and I wanted it and I had to have it, you
know, like I really needed it, my life depended on it.

S: That feeling that you had, that you had to get something,   40
was that a feeling that you had right from the beginning
of working on that or was it a feeling that developed as
you were working?

K: Yeah, it developed, 'cos first of all, like when we were
going to have a van, I thought, you know [shrugs] . . . I   45
don't know. It developed really. [Shrugs.]

S: Okay. Let's think about it in the way that you used your
bodies all the way through. Let's think of it in that
sense first of all and then later on we can think about
music and other things. Um. Could you say a little bit   50
about how either you individually, or the group as a
whole actually used themselves?

K: Well we sort of like, we expressed the way we felt, I
thought with our bodies, like we were stretching out
and trying to get hold of what was in front of us.   55

S: So there was stretching?

K: Yeah.

S: Anything else that was going on with those bodies,
apart from stretching?

K: Um [shrugs] . . . I don't . . . no.   60

S: After the, for example, the moment where the lights
were flashing there was a slow-motion sequence,
what was happening there with the various bodies as
it were?

K: Well, we were . . . I don't understand exactly what you   65
mean really.

Karen is at her most animated not in direct response to Stan's
questioning but where she describes what it felt like to move towards
the light (35–39). Here we begin to get a sense of her *personal*

engagement with the form. Her description entails a crescendo of intensifying feeling – 'wanted', 'had to have', 'really needed', 'my life depended on it' – one of the most powerful expressions of inspiration, eros, desire, that we encountered during the project. Stan somehow misses this compelling surge of feeling; instead he deflates her, and deflects her from any further re-engagement and exploration. His tendency and inclination is to talk about the group as a whole, from an external point of view, ignoring the animation and commitment that arises from her personal account of 'being there' – an account which for the first time makes her really 'present' in the conversation, oblivious of the camera. Stan redirects Karen's attention to practicalities. Karen has very little to offer in response, so he closes the subject.

Sensing Karen is at a loss Stan progresses his own agenda, raising the issue of 'body forms'. Karen is asked to 'say a little bit' on this area as if fulfilling a minimum requirement, providing a tick to fill a box. She describes (53–55) how the stretching out was an attempt to express through their bodies how she and the rest of the group felt. Implicit here are questions as to *what* they felt as they were stretching and what it was they were attempting to grasp – questions about the expression of feeling through form and the finding of form for feeling. Stan seems rather to want some sort of 'academic' explanation of the stretching sequence. His technical question (58–59), 'Anything else that was going on with those bodies apart from stretching?', is so abstracted from any particular movement (as feeling form) that Karen is bewildered and silenced, her momentary excitement lost. Having no sense of the fusion of feeling and form as central to Karen's transformative process, Stan is unable to engage her. Talk is used simply to provide static, random, fragmentary evidence that she has successfully appropriated technical skills.

In his comments after the conversation, Stan expressed a concern that some pupils might have difficulty with verbal response, and that too much might be expected of them: 'I never escaped from being the one who led the conversation. I obviously would wish to escape from that and make it a two-way process, but that's too much to ask of a 15 year old.' He makes the common mistake of attributing the limits of a child's verbal 'performance' to the child herself and overlooking the overwhelming part he might himself play in suppressing that performance. He displays no faith in the

authority and eloquence that derives from Karen's personal knowing, but rather sees knowledge in terms of appropriated skills,
techniques and dramatic content, of which he is the master.

It is regrettable that we managed to collect so little material in the
performing arts that would sustain this kind of analysis – especially
since we recognize that talk about performance raises particular
issues and difficulties, not least because the artwork in question
cannot literally be present. It has to be recalled by both partners in
the conversation and even then it is difficult for the pupil as performer
to take the perspective of the teacher as audience, and vice versa. The
use of video tape recording does not necessarily or automatically
resolve the problem since neither party may be able to connect the
experience they remember with what was recorded by the camera. At
best the recording will refresh or revive memories and might provide
a common point of reference, much as photographs can. As we go
on to point out at the end of case study 6, in assessing the performing
arts we must be clear of the pupil's relation to the work – as com-
poser, interpreter, performer and so on. We must be clear about the
sense in which the pupil *controlled the sensate material that embodied
her impulse*, the degree to which she had appropriated the 'text' to be
performed. For Stan, the drama teacher, and Karen, his pupil (GCSE
year 11), these problems are exacerbated – as they can be in the performing arts – by the fact that Karen has been working (i.e. composing and performing) as a member of a group. Most of the talk related
to drama in performance collected by the project focused either on
technical matters or on the moral/social message of the work.

The remaining case studies are experimental conversations conducted by Malcolm Ross. Louise is 15 and was selected by her art
teacher for Malcolm to talk with during one of the project's visits
to the school; Sally (24), a member of the research team, agreed to
work with Malcolm to explore the conversation concept; Jack (11)
is Malcolm's son.

Case study 5: Making a Long Face

Malcolm and Louise

The subject of this conversation is a life-size, (as yet) unglazed clay
head modelled by Louise, an eleventh-year pupil, as part of her art
GCSE coursework. Louise has also made a red wax face-mask of

Making a Long Face

the head to which she refers in passing. She talks to Malcolm in her school. She is meeting him for the first time and knows little about him except that he is a university lecturer and he wants to discuss her art work with her. Here we record the conversation in full (about 35 minutes in all), presenting it, as with the other examples, as extracts with accompanying commentaries. The sculpted head is positioned on a chair between the two speakers – rather awkwardly so that they have to twist to look at it. This set-up was dictated by the confines of the deputy head's office and the need to record the conversation on video.

M: Right, we're going to talk about, about her here.
L: *Her*. Yeah – I think that's better [i.e. calling the head 'her'].
M: So maybe you could tell me about her. I mean, describe her to me. What's there to say about her?
L: I think she's very different from what everybody else   5
  came up with.
M: Uhm.
L: I, I'll try . . . When I started doing it, our heads, and I
  didn't have any idea of what to do. On the telly I was
  watching, I think it was David Attenborough or   10
  someone like that, and it had African tribes and things
  and I just thought, 'Oh yeah, look at their noses,'
  because they've got tremendous noses and it just
  came from that, I think.
M: Yeah.   15
L: 'Cos I had absolutely no idea of what I was going to
  do with her. I just came back to school. It was
  something like African tribes or the Easter Islands or
  something like that.
M: Ah, yes.   20
L: And it just came from there.
M: So the project was to make a head?
L: Yeah. We started with portraits and then faces of
  people and then we could make a head of anything,
  whatever you wanted, and people had their own   25
  inspirations – some more serious than others.
M: And your inspiration, or the beginnings of it, was
  perhaps this television programme, these images
  that you saw there?
L: I really didn't know what to do. I was pottering   30
  around making all these different shapes and things
  that weren't going to lead anywhere, you know, for
  most of the term, and then it just suddenly developed
  and three weeks and it was finished.
M: So once you'd got that idea . . .   35

L: Yes.

M: Um! How, how did you go about it? I mean,
technically how did you go about it? I mean, did you . . .
you've got a mould there.

L: Yeah.   40

M: And has the mould . . . ? This has come out of the mould?

L: No, I made a clay head first with, like, a wooden
stand covered in cloth.

M: And then you moulded . . .

L: The clay over it, yeah, to make a head shape. And   .45
then I thought to make a mask or something. I wanted
the face on the mask so I made a cast of it, and then . . .

M: Off the clay?

L: Yeah, and then I thought I've got that and GCSE is
supposed to show the stages of it so I thought I'd do   50
well to have the back and the whole head so you
could see, you know, the stages of what development
there is. So, I don't know . . .

M: Right, so. This is now plaster?

L: It's glaze, I think.   55

M: This stuff? [Indicating its white, powdery surface.]

L: Yeah, it's a glaze. It's dipped in a glaze and then it's
fired . . .

M: What's under here? The clay?

L: The clay. I dipped it in the glaze and it'll be like stone   60
when it's fired.

M: Right, so this is now glaze?

L: Yeah.

M: I get you.

L: And it hasn't been fired yet. I think it's got to go in   65
really hot.

M: Yes. Is it solid?

L: Um, that? Yeah. It's a bit dirty because it hasn't been
fired, but . . .

M: It's not a hollow head?   70

L: No. Yeah! It's hollow inside because otherwise it
would blow up in the kiln. It's been fired originally but
it's just got to go in the kiln.

M: So it's had a biscuit firing?

L: I don't know what you call it, but it's there.   75

M: A *low* temperature firing. And now you've glazed it
   and it'll come out with a glossy finish?
L: I'm not sure whether it'll be glossy. I think it'll be stony.
   My teacher showed me some of other people's ones. I
   didn't really want, didn't think that glossy would go with 80
   it as much as . . .
M: Matt?
L: Yeah, it's more primitive, I think. So with my art history
   I've done some primitive art to go with it.
M: So it's making quite a nice project.   85
L: Yeah, I . . . It's different from, I think you call it,
   conventional art – Renaissance and all that kind of
   stuff – I thought I'd do something different. It interested
   me. I'm interested in it and I found it more interesting.
   It got me interested.   90

Much of this opening sequence – somewhat laboured as Malcolm
came to the work cold (and not well informed technically) – is
concerned with evidence of conventionalization (technique and
cultural contextual knowledge). Already, though, Louise has a sense
(5–6) of her head's difference 'from what everybody else came up
with' – this difference is pleasurable to her; it makes the art history
aspect to her project rather unusual: 'more interesting' (89).

Of greatest significance in this extract to the subsequent development of the conversation are the opening lines where the head comes
to be addressed as a 'her'. While the head was put in place for the
video Louise had flippantly insisted on its femaleness and Malcolm
took her seriously. His persistence in this, the opening move in the
conversation proper, encounters only momentary hesitation from
Louise. Malcolm has obviously taken a risk, but it is one which
pays off – by his naming the head 'her', the clay becomes the
potential site of depth constructs. As the conversation progresses
'she' acquires abstract as well as physical qualities: social, moral
and cultural meanings, character traits. 'She' becomes the starting
point of many different stories (meanings), some of which are
sustained throughout the conversation, others of which pass and
are forgotten.

At this stage all these possibilities are merely latent. What there
is to say about her (4) is very much already formulated public information, a coherent account of process and product. Since Malcolm

is unacquainted with Louise and with her set task, his curiosity is genuine and the exchange of questions and answers performs an important social function in orientating the two speakers towards one another, in establishing a rapport and a tone. Addressing the head as 'her' also has something of this function in its inherent playfulness.

Many of our conversations contain little more than is covered in this single extract. In this case, this is only a beginning.

M: It's interesting that you're saying that in about three
    weeks it all suddenly came together – what you
    wanted to do. When you began, did you have these –
    'the Easter Island heads' – or whatever it was, in mind?
L: No I didn't. I was thinking... when I finished I thought   100
    'Yeah, that looks quite similar to that.'
M: Did you do a doodle? Do you know what I mean?
    Did you just play around with eyes and noses and
    things?
L: Yeah.   105
M: So really without any clear design in mind?
L: I did, once I'd played around with things and
    sketched out how I was going to have it, like, in the
    end, and worked from that partly, and then changed it
    because it looked silly or whatever, or didn't work   110
    three-dimensionally. But I think I had a quite definite
    picture of how I wanted the nose to be.
M: The nose is very significant.
L: Yeah it is. I was amazed, like watching the telly,
    coloured people and their noses are so much bigger   115
    than ours – different shapes – and I was just amazed
    really – quite strange.

Here Malcolm selects from the conversation so far the part of Louise's account of process in which she appears to describe the onset of her inspiration (30–34): meandering progression, a sudden focus followed by swift resolution. He is curious to know more about what happened here, when out of directionless pottering Louise suddenly found a direction. Technical processes seem to have little relevance here – the concern is with evolving shapes, forms, ideas, feelings, intimations. In returning to this area, recalling more closely the imaginative and sensory processes, Louise recovers material that proves crucial to the present contemplation: 'But I think I had quite a definite picture of how I wanted the nose to be' (111–112).

Malcolm hears the conviction in Louise's comment and echoes it with a positive response of his own: 'The nose is very significant.' His remark is in the present tense, indicating her success in realizing her desire in the finished form. Malcolm is established as an *actively engaged observer* who will partner Louise in her perceptions and interpretations of the head, while allowing for the uniqueness of her relation to it. His sense of the 'nose' as significant seems to spring from the immediacy of his own growing percipience. 'Significant' is both a surface and a depth construct: it relates to the physical size of the nose, the way it fits with other features in the face; but it also suggests that the nose 'signifies', that it is invested with meaning. The meaning, as yet unexplored, is embodied both in the objective physical thing and somehow in Louise. If the process of publication is a clarifying and conscious realization of meaning and of the simultaneous connectedness and separateness of the objective form and subjective forming, then Malcolm's comment is a kind of permission for this to take place. Co-presence is a condition of publication.

M: Tell me about that face [circles hand by head]. It's a
   very unusual face. Is it a face or a head?
L: It's a head [looking at M, then round back of head].   120
M: Right. Tell me about that head [leaning back, his arms
   crossed].
L: I think it's a bit morbid, sad-looking, especially around
   the eyes and the cheeks [indicating with hand, looking
   across at M and back at head].   125
M: Yeah.
L: It's not frightening [rocking back and forth, looking]. I
   think it's just sad. It's not as if it's going to be on a post
   to frighten somebody off. It's not like that, it's [pause]
   . . . I don't really know. [Pause. Leans forward,   130
   shifting her head about.]
M: Is the nose sad?
L: I don't know that the nose is so much sad [leans right
   back]. Well, I think it could be in the way that it's
   curving [gestures this to M]–it's quite a sad . . . and   135

the mouth is [*M* uncrosses his arms, leans right forward
to peer] really tight [looking down at head again].

M: Yes.

L: It [hesitantly], it looks a lot more sorrowful in the clay
[gestures in front of head] than it does in the wax, in   140
the cast [glances towards cast; *M* leans back, arms
crossed]. I think to . . .

M: More sorrowful.

L: More sorrowful, yeah. I think it's just the shape of the
head [gesturing with both hands to own head] and   145
the very long faced [moves hands down her face].
'Feel sorry for myself today' [speaks in 'her' voice].

The conversation begins to move now into a second phase, where
the head becomes the entirely present focus of attention and is
explored as both surface and depth.

Malcolm's contributions are minimal here. He first directs
Louise's looking towards her piece, seeking clarification as to how
to define it (the head is not explicitly a 'she' here) and then simply
indicates that he is listening, waiting and himself pondering. His
stance seems to encourage Louise to dwell on her perceptions; at
each turn she elaborates, looks again, finds reasons *in the piece*
to confirm her sense of its sorrow. *There is constant movement
between surface and depth.* At line 130 her words, 'I don't really
know,' are not an expression of hopelessness or closure, but are
more ruminative, the grounds for renewed looking and consideration. Malcolm's question, 'Is the nose sad?', helps her to achieve a
closer focus by suggesting that the feeling she detects may be found
in particular elements of the form. Louise easily responds to this,
modifying her thought as she looks. Her discovery of the sad curve
is an eloquent embodiment of feeling in form. Her perception of
the clay as more sorrowful than the wax (144–146) intensifies this
further, discriminating the elements of texture and body and surface
as well as shape.

At the end of the extract (147) a further transformation takes
place: the head 'speaks': 'Feel sorry for myself today.' It is as if
the sorrow that Louise first saw in the piece – 'It's a bit morbid,
sad-looking' (123) – has become so closely identified with its
individual forms and features that it has now become an element of
personality: being so intensely looked at, the piece comes to life.

This occurs several times in the conversation as, during the processes of publication, the piece takes on a life of its own. Giving it speech, Louise makes it quite definitely 'other', another participant in the conversation. But her personification is essentially playful.

M: Uhm. What else could you say about her? [Leans
forward to look.] I wanted to say, is this a death mask?
Do you know what a death mask is?   150
L: What they used to put on faces when they're dead?
M: Yes, well it's an impression taken from a dead person
and then just as you made a face from that head – there
are some very famous death masks, aren't there?
L: Yeah, yeah.   155
M: Doesn't it have that feeling about it?
L: Yeah, yeah. I think it does, you know . . . very . . .
M: This is an impression of someone who has lived as
against a portrait of a living person. Has this person
died, is what I'm really saying?   160
L: Yeah, it's sort of true . . . not, er . . .
M: I mean, you're talking about your imagination, your
feelings for her.
L: I think, yeah, she's no longer in there.
M: No.   165
L: Yeah, I think she has. Yeah, definitely she hasn't got
the liveness in shaping and forms . . . like . . . you
saw Fiona's, didn't you, with a moustache?
M: Yeah, yeah.
L: Hers is very alive – the character in the eyes, and   170
shapes – I think that's good, but . . . it's quite cold.
M: Yes.
L: [Pause.] I haven't really looked at her and said what I think.
You know, I don't really know.

Having listened attentively to Louise, Malcolm's contribution now increases as he introduces the idea of the death mask. This is a kind of test, which offers Louise a new interpretation of what the form represents. It firmly reintroduces the notion of the head as a 'she', gathering with it possibilities for story. The question, 'Has this person died?', involves an acceptance of the head as more than the combination of the formal elements which evoke feelings in the looker, but which have no referent. Here a living person, a life history is being connoted. At lines 162–163 Malcolm explicitly 'permits' Louise to explore in this way with 'your imagination, your feelings' but she in fact needs little encouragement, stating easily, 'I think, yeah, she's no longer in there,' and substantiating this in 'shaping and forms', while drawing a comparison with a friend's work.

Louise does more than appropriate the idea of the death mask from Malcolm, she begins to transform it through her own sensate ordering. This process continues as she goes on looking, her responses always finding justification in the physicality of the piece, in the form which is the trace of her forming.

At the end of the extract Louise registers her sense that she is being asked here to address her work in an unfamiliar way. She feels herself on slightly shaky ground, not sure perhaps of how legitimate her responses are or how to provide them. For a time, the actual exploration is suspended, while the conversation partners reflect on what they have been doing.

> L: [Pause.] I haven't really looked at her and said what
>   I think, You know, I don't really know.
> M: But you're doing it now?   175
> L: Yes.
> M: How does it feel to be doing it?
> L: [Pause.] That's . . .
> M: I mean, does it feel wrong to be doing it?
> L: No, no, no! It's stimulating my imagination, which is   180
>   good.
> M: I mean, you made her . . . very much with your
>   hands and your eyes without reflecting too much.
> L: Yes.
> M: Almost, I suspect, that sort of even unconsciously   185
>   you've gone on making her and said, 'This is right
>   now and . . .
> L: Yes.
> M: . . . that's not quite balanced. I like that colour, I'll have
>   a bit more like that.' Now we've got her. So it was like   190
>   that?
> L: Yeah.
> M: We're trying to say, 'What have we got? What have we
>   found?' It's like you've been . . .

L: Been to a psychiatrist! 195

M: Well, I don't know! That strikes me as something like
a *morbid* experience. I'm just saying, no, what have
we found? You've gone fishing, you've gone deep-
sea diving, you've gone into a wreck – I'm now using
a kind of metaphor for your making process. You've 200
gone down there, glided, groped around, you've
made it, you've come up, you've brought her up, and
here she is. Now, who, what have we got here? And
what does she mean? Because, she, I mean, *does*
she mean something for you? I don't know, does . . . I 205
mean does she have any value for you [gesturing
towards the head]?

Louise recognizes, by her joking mention of the psychiatrist
(195), the particularly personal tenor of the conversation, but at
the same time she does not see it as intrusive. Malcolm offers an
extended metaphor which locates the present activity as a natural
continuation of the making processes that have gone before. The
diving metaphor encapsulates the movement through appropriation, transformation and publication. The three are crucially linked:
you can't surface without having dived; surfacing 'completes' the
dive.

Louise clearly accepts this description and promptly answers
Malcolm's question as to value with a striking perception, which she
is herself surprised by and which initiates an intense period of
imaginative discovery.

M: Now, who, what have we got here? And what does
she mean? Because, she, I mean, *does* she
mean something for you? I don't know, does . . . I mean 205
does she have any value for you [gesturing towards
the head]?

L: I think she's quite regal.

M: [excitedly] Ah yes! [Sits back, folds arms.] I
mean *I* do. I wanted you to say and I didn't want to 210
put words into your mouth [leans to look at head and
then up at *L*], but I have a tremendous sense of her
dignity. Because I think she has a . . .

L: I've just found that!

M: Have you? 215

L: Yes! Something to do [puts hand to own face] with
    the shape of her here [touches the head and own face
    in same place, sits back and looks] – the shadows
    and her jaw [indicates own jaw, M sits on edge
    of seat] – very stiff [M anticipates this description,   220
    making a long-face gesture with hands and face,
    L watching him], very . . . Queen, Victoria or . . . I don't
    know.

M: Yep. [Nods.]

L: Stiff, quietly sitting by her husband, being told, or the   225
    other way round. 'Everybody under my, under my little
    thumb.' [Hesitant, looking back at the head.]

M: Yes [looking]. She looks so forbidding and do you
    know I can imagine her . . . I can imagine her, smiling.

L: Humpf [amused, cocks head to look from new angle].   230
    Yeah.

M: She's not smiling, I mean, she's not smiling now
    [leans back, resting forehead on arm], but I can imagine
    her smile. [L watching head.] I can imagine her
    opening those eyes and I think I would like her to   235
    look at me.

L: Yeah, she's not looking you in the face. [Looks up at M.]

M: She's not. If she were to look at me [looking at L; L
    looking at head], I mean I would want her to look at
    me. I'd want her to notice . . .   240

L: If she looked at you she'd smile [looking directly at M].

M: She *would* smile and and I think she – I would like
    to be looked at by a woman like that [L looking at
    head all the time] is what I'm saying.

L: [Laughs up at M.] Hiding away, isn't she?   245

M: She's not available. No, I think she's . . .

L: No. Knock on her shell! [Mimes, laughing.]

M: Yeah, well you said she wasn't in there.

L: Yeah, yeah.

M: I think maybe, I don't know, maybe, she isn't in there. 250

L: It's a death mask.

M: Yes, but it's terrific, isn't it? We're saying that as
    we're looking at her there's a great richness in her
    and . . .

L: Yeah, I never noticed it.   255

M: . . . in what you've made there.
L: Yeah.

Again Louise's discovery, 'I've just found that!,' is grounded in her surface perceptions (214). Her gestures are an eloquent part of the way she communicates with Malcolm, moving from the clay head to her own face. Malcolm echoes and acknowledges her animation with gestures of his own. It is almost as if the image has become detached from the object – fuelled by perception, the imagination 'takes off'.

It is not through exact equivalence that the head acquires 'presence' but through the quality of suggestion. The head does not become Queen Victoria (222), but it *evokes* her, brings her into being (225–227) as a whole figure, with a husband, quietly voicing her command: 'Everybody under my, under my little thumb.'

The flow of Louise's attention is lateral, oscillating between the single real object and imaginary objects. The sculpted head has become what Barthes (1986) has called 'the infinitely available site of subjective investments'.

Malcolm agrees with Louise's image, how she has communicated the head as 'forbidding' (228) and then goes on to offer an imagining of his own: 'I can imagine her, smiling' (229). This is imagining of a slightly different kind, giving the head itself, 'her', the potential of a past and a future, a narrative possibility, which before was deflected through the suggestion of Queen Victoria. Malcolm's idea returns to the physical features of the head: her mouth, her eyes. It is these which now must be transformed by their willing, attentive imagination. This sense of the imagination as an active creative force is conveyed by the exercise of desire on Malcolm's part: 'I think I would like her to look at me' (235–236), 'I mean, I would want her to look at me' (239–240), 'I would like to be looked at by a woman like that' (242–243). The object can be worked on by the desiring imagination, can be rendered fluid, given life. Notice the way the shaped fantasy develops easily between the two speakers. They pick up, affirm and further each other's contributions so that the dialogue (232–251) becomes almost seamless. They start with the possibility of her smiling and end up with the image of the death mask: both life and death are contained here; openness, warmth and retreat, retirement, withdrawal, distance; fullness, emptiness. These oppositions recur continuously in the conversation. They are evoked very naturally here in the form of dialogue where the focus and mode of attention is shared. The polarities are fused in the texture of the verbal exchange itself, which is generous and engaged.

Clinching the exchange with animated summary ('Yes, but it's terrific, isn't it?'), Malcolm evaluates not what has been said but its quality – the 'great richness in her' is discovered through such talk, through such imagining. As it is generated it is found: Louise says, 'Yeah, I never noticed it.'

M: When you say you haven't noticed, is that right?
L: Not consciously, no – I might've – in there [taps her head].
M: Unconsciously.   290
L: Yeah.
M: Well, I think when one makes something like this,
    when you doodle anyway, when you just doodle,
    there's a lot of unconscious work going on there, isn't
    there? And it's sometimes quite interesting to see   295
    what you've got. So you've come up with various
    things and you're saying that she's dignified – well,
    you didn't – you're saying 'amazing nose'. And her
    nose *is* amazing, there's no doubt about it!
L: I like it. I think I've got a thing about noses. My   300
    Grandpa has a tremendous nose.
M: He has a big nose, too, does he?
L: It's like a strawberry. It's . . . I don't know . . . And my cousin
    and my brother have got miniature versions of it and
    they're growing bigger and . . . [laughs].   305
M: So you . . . do you like your Grandpa?
L: Yes.
M: So does he look like his nose? Like Grandpa, like
    his nose?
L: Yeah, it goes with him. It's so funny . . . He's my best 310
    Grandpa.

This is a kind of breathing space in the conversation, a coming up for air, an opportunity as before to reflect on and thereby to legitimize what is going on. It could be a point of closure, Malcolm summarizing what has been discovered, but instead it is a point of new departure, Louise talking confidently now about her very personal fascination, her 'thing about noses' (300), her Grandpa, how comic the family resemblances are to her. This is fond, anecdotal information, revealing very personal ways of seeing and sensing, which derive from unique memories and associations. It comes across as pleased informal chat conveying a sense of ease and confidence in the conversation. Sociability affirmed, Malcolm returns to the imaginative exploration of the piece, Louise effortlessly following and developing his train of thought. The different levels of attention and forms of engagement within the 'whole' of the conversation enrich and support one another, building not only aesthetic meanings but a real and living relationship between the two speakers, who, only minutes before, had been total strangers.

M: Best Grandpa. Okay. I'm saying that I find her, I find a
   lot in her – and contrary to her austere and even
   forbidding and even to the fact that this may be
   a death mask, she may have gone. This may have   315
   been, in our imagination we could say that this may
   have been made on her after . . .
L: You could see someone lying there, couldn't you?
M: Yes. Despite all those things, I'm saying that I sense
   her vitality, her humour, I sense that I would want her   320
   if she were alive to look at me and look at me with, I
   mean, even love or affection or respect. I'd want to
   belong to her.
L: Yup, I think, just talking now, I think she is a her . . .
   I don't think I could see her as a . . . I think she's a her. 325
M: Yes, well, you corrected me right at the beginning,
   didn't you, about that?
L: That's just because, you know, a car's always a her,
   so why can't she be a her?
M: But now she is a HER?   330
L: Yes, she definitely is [leaning to peer round the back
   of the head]. There's something about the structure of . . .
   I didn't spend much time on it, but I can see from the
   shadows [looking and gesturing at the back of the
   head; M leans to look], the structure of her here . . . her 335
   jaw, down here [moving hands around from head to
   own face, looking from different angles]. I can't think
   where it came from now . . . I was just doodling around
   with something. And a friend of mine, when he shouts

> he's got a really pronounced jaw-bone, and I was   340
> thinking, seeing if I could get it, and it works quite
> well with her . . . in-cut down here.
> M: Yes . . . Yes. You've got her jaw-bone.
> L: It's so much there. I don't think a lot of it was planned.
> M: No.   345
> L: It just came.

Here it is as if Malcolm is working with the vitality and humour that Louise has evoked about her grandpa and herself and is making them components of *his* story about the head, feeding them spontaneously into his engagement with it, his depth constructs. Malcolm orientates himself towards Louise; he listens and responds, channelling his response through the clay form which is the object of their joint contemplation. Similarly Louise, unprompted, orientates herself to Malcolm's new comments. While recognizing the relevance of personal history and anecdote to her making, they perceive the head with detachment, as distinct, separate. As an open site of meaning the head comes to mean, through interaction. *Publication is embedded in the dialogic form of the conversation itself.*

The richness of Malcolm's description, his statement of personal connection – 'I'd want to belong to her' (322–323) – is followed by Louise's strong affirmation of the head's femaleness: the possibility she had before been playfully entertaining has become a conviction. Again, characteristically, her belief is grounded in a renewed investigation of the head's sensate qualities (332–336). Her direct perceptual engagement recalls her making processes, the 'doodling around' and the echoes of a friend. Throughout (331–342), Louise's gestures intensify and confirm the expression of her words; she is both sensing and thinking aloud, making connections and wondering at the structural qualities she discerns. Established knowledge (the making process) is revivified, made dynamic by new perceiving.

> M: You've assembled . . . She's got possibly Grandfather's
>   nose and the boyfriend's jaw.
> L: [Laughs.] I don't know about that.
> M: She's got bits.   350
> L: She's got me in the morning – droopy . . .
> M: I was going to ask you about that. Has she got . . . I
>   don't know quite what I'm asking but, um . . . Do you
>   think in some way, not that she looks like you, but that

on, um... Is this the kind of thing you are glad to make? 355
Do you say, 'That's *my* kind of thing'? Or is it just any
old thing? Is it your kind of thing in some kind of
special way? People say . . . well, I don't know . . . 'Certain
textures are me.'

L: Yeah, the things I stand for? 360

M: Uhm.

L: Yeah I do.

M: So does she belong to you in that sort of way?

L: There's a lot of me in her, yeah. Uhm, definitely.
People think I'm what I am but I'm not what I am. I'm 365
not saying I put it on but, you know, everyone thinks,
'Louise is funny, doesn't mind. Anyone can say
anything to her and she'll laugh,' but, you know, I'm
not really like that.

M: There's another side of you which not everybody 370
knows.

L: I wouldn't say it was a sad side.

M: No. I'm not saying she looks like you or anything
like that.

L: I hope not! 375

M: It's almost like your signature. Is she yours in the way
that your signature is you in some way? You choose . . .
There are certain . . . there are times when you choose
your own clothes. You say, 'Well, that's me. That's
how I like to be. That's how I see myself. That's my 380
way of doing things.' Is this your way of doing things
in some way, in some sense?

L: In some ways.

M: Are you the author of this? I know you made her but
are you her author, are you her . . . 385

L: Yeah, I do. Yeah, I think so. Not . . . I didn't go out and
say . . . You know, I say I can see her, all these stories –
they didn't even cross my mind until my teacher said
that it was primitive and I thought, 'Well, fair enough.'
I can see it now but when I was making it . . . 390

M: You didn't have the Easter Island . . . ?

L: No!

M: Or anything like that at all?

L: No, nothing like that.

The authenticity of the piece is addressed here – quite a difficult area since it demands that the connection between the maker and her object becomes her focus of attention. The piece is momentarily not out in the world but is demanding of commitment: is it 'my kind of thing' or 'just any old thing'? Louise is light-hearted, self-mocking. She is happy with her surface affability (364–369) but at the same time is conscious of and is confident in a more serious side to her nature ('the things I stand for'). Making this connection with herself seems important. It allows her to put aside (386–390) the Easter Island idea (in part her teacher's) with which she started the conversation and to begin to sense how she might own the piece in a personal and particular way. The period of conversation that follows is full of discoveries and excitement. Depth counters dominate as her 'real presence' is evoked:

M: [leaning back, looking at L] And she actually came   395
much more from your . . .

L: From underneath [looking at head].

M: Your playing and the nose. This idea that I'll build a
face around a nose – this great big nose.

L: Yeah, I did actually. [Looks at M and across at head.]   400
I thought 'I want a huge big nose on this'. [Pauses,
looking.] Strange person! Fascinated with noses!
[Laughs; M grinning.]

M: Well, it's, what about that? I mean, what did that
fascination do for this making? [L staring out window,   405
thinking] This particular making?

L: It's given it some character, hasn't it? [Looks at head.]

M: Yeah.

L: And it's given her length in the face which she
wouldn't have had [gesturing up and down].   410

M: No [pause]. Is she foreign, alien, strange?
[Leaning back, relaxed.]

L: [adamant] No, I don't think so. [Looking from different
angles.] She might not be Cornish, or English, but
she's not from another planet [i.e. an alien].   415

M: So you can respond to her humanity?

L: Yeah. I think she's very much humanity [looking up
at M]. And a principled person.

M: Principles? [Grins, sits back, changes to more

comfortable sitting position, folds arms.]   420
L: Yes I think so [smiling at *M*].
M: Go on, because I'm seeing something else now too.
L: Yeah [scratches her head, pleased, bit embarrassed],
    she's got my views on racism and things like that and
    the environment.   425
M: What other issues? [Inclines head enquiringly.] What
    are her views on these things?
L: I think it's probably why she's got the nose [staring at
    head], you know. She seems very upset [looks at
    M] at the way people carry on – politicians – and   430
    it has to take so long to do something. It's what
    it says. It's, I think it's quite a negro nose.
    You don't find many white people with a nose
    like that.
M: No.   435
L: It's very flat.
M: I'm wondering why you say . . . I mean, I think you're
    right but . . . And it may be that we can't explain it . . .
L: [simultaneously] You don't know how you get to it,
    do you?   440
M: . . . the notion that you sense her values are your
    values and that . . . I thought you said, 'These values are
    my values but somehow they're caught up in that nose.'
L: Yeah.
M: That nose, somehow or other [*L* laughs] – yes –   445
    embodies those values or evokes those values or
    suggests those values to you. You're saying she had
    great principles, didn't you – regal? Um, do you feel
    she has suffered?

Attention turns again to the nose. This, it seems, is Louise's signature: 'Strange person! Fascinated with noses!' The nose is the piece's 'holding form' (Witkin 1974) – it is responsible for 'character' (407) (depth construct) and for structure ('length in the face' (409) – surface construct); for feeling and for form. All else falls into place around it.

'Is she foreign, alien, strange?' (411): though founded in ideas and hints that appeared before, Malcolm's question is a new and direct stimulus. Louise's response is clear; she defends 'her' from being classed as 'from another planet' (415) and Malcolm helps her interpret her sense of her humanity. Accepting this she bestows the head with moral meaning: she is 'a principled person' (418).

The conversation here evokes a great sense of 'presentness' and of 'presence': 'she' has principles because Louise sees and decides *now* that she has. Malcolm is engaged, wants to know more, thinks he may be on a similar track himself. His curiosity is vital, aroused both by Louise and by his own perceptions of the physical image. There is a sense of fun, pleasure and adventure here. A mutual trust is at work, a complementarity, a complementing of one another. These are important qualities of publication. The physical presence of the head is referred to continually by look and gesture; it remains constant and central, the place where Louise's flights of fantasy are anchored. There is no clearer sense of this than when, asked by Malcolm 'What are her views on these things?', she replies, 'I think it's probably why she's got the nose' (426–428). Surface and depth are no longer distinguishable, the form is saturated with feeling (see the comment in Chapter 3). Louise goes on to say, 'She seems very upset at the way people carry on – politicians – and it has to take so long to do something' (429–431). The sense is of human values imperilled by forces that refuse to listen. The powerful personality which the head embodies is circumstantially impotent; remember the sad curve of the nose, her withdrawal inside her shell.

Malcolm is listening hard, *interpreting*, trying to help Louise to go further.

M: . . . Um, do you feel she has suffered?
L: [pause] She certainly looks like it [Laughs.] Um, I   450
    think the way she looks at the moment, I think she has.
    Yeah. I think she, you know . . .
M: She may have had an anguished death, are you
    saying?
L: Yeah. I don't know whether an anguished death but   455
    regretting something.
M: Um. What would that be? As her author you could
    know, or you might know, or you could guess.
L: Well, missed out on an opportunity or hasn't done
    something. Regretted something that happened. [L   460
    looking at head, M leans forward to look.]
M: Is she very old?

L: [pause] Middle-aged I would say . . . I don't know.
[Shifts round in seat.] Misshapen isn't she? [Leans
head on arm.] She could be old, mentally old [sits up   465
again].

M: She looks as if she's had a bit of an accident at some
point [leaning forward, pointing].

L: [Laughs.] Yeah [leans down, head on hand again],
this side's a bit . . .   470

M: A flatness here [both almost touching head], which is
strange, isn't there [leans back]?

L: Yeah – and on this as well [gestures].

M: Now she seems as if she's been through it a bit.

L: I think she's quite old [pauses]. Yeah I do. I think   475
she's more likely to be old than middle-aged.
[Leaning right back, looking round back of head.]

M: Do you feel satisfied? Are you satisfied in yourself
with her?

L: Yeah I'm quite pleased with her. Yeah. [Sits back.]   480
Yeah, I am, actually. I could have worked a lot more
on the actual shapes round here [indicating with
cupped hand] but it wouldn't be her if I'd have done
that now – it would have been [voice drops] things
that affected her a bit, you know. She wouldn't be,   485
she wouldn't have that look about her [smiles], she
wouldn't be so, she wouldn't [sits up, looks at M]
have so much dignity if she were so smooth and
perfect. [Pause.] I'm enjoying this – it's stimulating,
really good!   490

Louise's head has no simple, singular or generalized meaning
abstractable from its physical presence; it has no depth without
surface. Louise demonstrates this again and again; for her *there is
no knowing without perceiving*. And since perceiving is always
new, always recent – she never tires of looking – her knowing has
to it a potentiality and a potency; it is never closed, never complete.

The above extract shows the freedom with which Louise makes
revisions as a result of her looking, imagination and experience. Her
sense of 'regretting something' (456) prompts Malcolm to wonder
how old 'she' is (462). Louise ventures first to say that she is middle-
aged but, testing this against her perceptions – 'Misshapen, isn't

she?' – she revises this first simply to 'old', then refining this further to 'mentally old'. She achieves a subtle sense of what age means and how it manifests itself. It is not measured in years only, but also in experience: it is through experience that we come to know regret. Mental oldness – a depth construct – concerned with the interior private world is manifested physically in curves and shapes. Feeling is not locked away but shows itself in form. Equally the form is seen as the origin of the feeling. There is no real distinction, each contains the other.

Asked whether she feels satisfied with her work, Louise again re-engages with the form (480–490), reflecting back on her technical making processes, only to reject them as largely irrelevant to what – and who – the piece now is. She arrives at another striking insight, 'She wouldn't have so much dignity if she were so smooth and perfect.' Her constructs ('perfect–imperfect', 'dignity–lack of dignity') fuse to convey the complex sense that, for Louise, the dignity of self manifests itself in the imperfection of form. The imperfection of form indicates experience ('regret', 'things that affected her a bit') and age. It is a kind of truth, how the deterioration of the physical corresponds to the perfection of the spiritual (it is both ideal and terrible at the same time). Louise later describes the head as warm and bitter.

> L: I'm enjoying this – it's stimulating, really good!
> M: What are we doing?
> L: Using the imagination.
> M: Ah. [Pause.] And it's all . . . I mean, we're not putting anything on top, are we?
> L: Building on it.   495
> M: Are we getting inside what you've been doing?
> L: Yeah, I think so.
> M: I mean, not in a nosy kind of way.
> L: No, I'm trying to find out . . .
> M: Open a few windows, let some light in on the process   500
>   – that is obviously a very complex process.
> L: Uhm. I suppose because it was done at school. You have an hour and ten minutes once a week to do it and you get into the routine. And I think she hasn't got that rigidness that you have in school.   505
> M: Where did she come from? You made her in school . . .

L: But where does she come from though?

M: But you . . . I mean, literally you had to make her in those hour-and-a-half sessions.

L: Yes. That's probably why I didn't get on to anything to   510
start with, you know, because of work . . .

M: You mean, you didn't get any . . .

L: Yeah, it takes . . . Once you get going you think 'Ahh',
and then the bell goes and it's science next, you
know. And then once I got the idea I just shut up and   515
did it and got it done. And once I got my interest in it
and knew I'm going now and I'm interested, that's it!
There's something to spark you off to start with, and,
you know, you're an artist . . .

M: That feeling.   520

L: Yeah, you can't sit down. And sometimes you go and
you just can't produce something worth producing.
You've got to be in the right frame of mind to do . . .

M: That frame of mind doesn't have anything to do with
having a title, does it?   525

L: No, it's just . . . I don't know. Sometimes it's got to be
relaxed and quiet and I look forward to it when I'm
like that – I'm going to do it. If I have a bad day I
normally do that. It sounds so stupid. If you've had a
bad day and it's going well, it's so nice. In school art   530
isn't . . . a subject you can do, because you're doing it
off your own bat because you're enjoying it and wanting
to [interruption as other pupils enter the room] . . .
Getting off the subject a bit?

The partners surface a little and reflect first on the activity they
have been engaged in and then more generally on the constraints of
doing art in school. Again this is supportive, confidential talk,
not really 'off the subject' because it contextualizes the experience.

Finally, Malcolm introduces a new sort of approach. He takes a
more leading role, but this is only when the conversation is far
advanced and when the arrival of other pupils in the interview
room means that it must shortly be drawn to a close. He ventures
a different play.

M: Well, not really. I think it's part of what we've been   535

> trying to say. Um. [Pause.] If I, I'm going to ask you a
> sort of crazy question now Um. What is . . . can you
> think of some . . . is she warm, is she cold? Is she
> sharp, is she blunt? Is she rough, is she smooth? Is
> she bitter, is she sweet? Can you think of those sorts   540
> of things? Tastes and sounds.
>
> L: She's warm [quietly, looking].
> M: She's warm.
> L: Bitter somewhere.
> M: And there's a bitterness there.   545
> L: Yeah. I think.
> M: That's an interesting mix, isn't it?
> L: Yeah. Not very bitter [gesturing at head]. Just a bit.
> M: All right, you touched on that. Not so as to destroy her
>   dignity, because she hasn't suddenly gone mean.   550
> L: No, she looks [mumbles]. She's, um, compassionate.
> M: That's warmth. I think that's why I want her to look at
>   me. I think she'd understand.
> L: Yes, understand. [Cocks head.] If she opened her
>   eyes ... [commands head] 'Open your eyes!' You could   555
>   just give her a prod [mimes, laughing] and wake her
>   up, couldn't you? [M grinning in response.] [Pause.]
>   She's warm in a sense of being [grasps hands
>   together, gestures; M sits forward] which – I don't
>   know [slapping hands down on lap].   560

Malcolm introduces the idea of sensate constructs – as whole
units, and used as the tools rather than the outcomes of exploration.
In lines 537–541, he presents, by way of examples, a selection of
possible answers. In the light of her previous discoveries Louise
has no difficulty selecting words and supplying more of her own.
The head is both warm and bitter (a synaesthetic compound). She
is 'compassionate'(551) – a metaphorical understanding of 'warm' –
which revives Louise's sense of the head as characterful and causes
her to command it, playfully to demand a response. The movement
implied in 'metaphor' is significant here: a way of relating surface to
depth, one thing to another in a new whole. 'She' is warm because
she is compassionate, 'she's warm in a sense of being' (558), but she
also resists being woken up, she is withdrawn.

> M: [squinting] Are there any others which would do for
>   her? Is she smooth? Is she still or is she running?

L: Still [moves hand across head], kind of graceful.

M: Yeah. So those are kind of qualities in her [gesturing at *L*] and in this I think [gesturing towards head]. 565

L: Yes. You can tell when she was little she was made to walk with a book on her head [gestures, smiles] or something, the way . . .

M: Yes, maybe that's what I meant by suffering. I think she's actually been [draws himself up, hands at 570 chest] . . .

L: Made to [folds hands primly on lap, in response to *M*'s gesture] . . .

M: . . . trained in some way, hasn't she? She's actually had to submit to a regime [flings arms forward], but 575 my goodness me, those eyes of hers, whatever they are, are wonderful.

L: Uhm [bit doubtful], I don't know [Scratches forehead.] I can't quite picture her with eyes.

M: No? [Leans back.] 580

L: I can – I expect when she opens her eyes [hand up to face; *M* leans forward] I can see her smile coming up [lifts hands] as I said earlier and changing her and, I don't know, maybe laugh a lot.

M: Yeah. 585

L: The things we said before [looks at *M*] I don't really know all the words to describe her.

M: But a lot of richness there.

L: Uhm.

Malcolm introduces more sensate constructs and Louise responds easily, but is not confined by the game; she moves easily from surface to depth, from 'still' to 'graceful' (563) to an imaginative projection into 'her' childhood training. Malcolm instantly makes a connection with the earlier notion of suffering and the two launch into a kind of dance, each reciprocating the movements of the other to convey their shared insight. As they take on in their gestures the imagined character of the head, 'she' almost begins to have a body!

It is a significant moment in the publication process when Louise says that she, unlike Malcolm, 'can't quite picture her with eyes': it is honest and confident, suggesting both her ease in the conversation and her true sense of ownership. It is subtly discriminating too. Louise begins to convey this very private particular meaning which makes itself known as a doubt, a sensing of not-quite-rightness. For her, the smile is more significant – and more accessible – than the eyes, which would perhaps be too engaging, too searching if one were to be looked at by them. When she thinks of 'looking', Louise thinks of a smile breaking out, demonstrating that warmth and compassion, 'changing her' (583) but, perhaps, not giving so much of her away as her eyes might do.

Time runs out, other roles and duties begin to make themselves felt and the search for 'all the words to describe her' comes to an end, though it could almost certainly have gone on and yielded further rewards. In contrast to the neatly closed explanation for the piece offered at the beginning of the conversation, Louise concludes with rich inexactitude. Through the activity of publication, her experience of herself and of her making have been transformed. In the closing exchanges, the head – 'she' – is assured an unequivocal place of value. The wheel has come full circle and conventionalization is both spontaneous and thoroughly justified.

M: Great, well, now you've quite enjoyed this   590
    conversation, didn't you?

L: Yeah, I have done. It's more educational. I've learnt a lot about her and about me and you know, how I came about her, I didn't know, it just happened [gesturing, smiling].

M: That you weren't aware of. Back there [indicating back of his head] somewhere?

L: Uhm. She means a lot more to me now than she did before. Yes, I think I would've been more upset if I broke her because of my GCSE work, whereas now,   600
she's – I want to get her home and have her sitting in the corner of my bedroom [gestures, smiling broadly, out towards camera].

Case study 6: Joining the Dance

Malcolm and Sally

Sally (aged 24), a member of the research team, talks to Malcolm about her participation in a day of dance. She had never been involved in such a project before. The task set for the participants by the course director was to work in domestic rooms, using simple routines from daily life evoked by the locations, to suggest ideas for a dance. Sally worked with an equally inexperienced partner, Liz. The conversation – in two parts, taking probably well over an hour altogether – took place about two months after the dance day. It brings a number of issues concerning arts assessment through talk into focus.

The previous case study clearly demonstrated the formative role of the adult's response. Malcolm's active attention both to the art object and to Louise as its maker acted as an important touchstone for her, supporting her growing percipience, confidence and sense of the piece's meaning and value: it was a manifestation of praise. Interest, curiosity, attentiveness and arousal are all manifestations of praise; they are formative; they build, stimulate, motivate, facilitate satisfaction. This is an important lesson about assessment: in order to value, the pupil must herself feel valued. Louise was able to appraise her piece, and through her piece, to appraise herself; crucially, her self-appraisal was based upon shared appraisal. Praise has always been understood as an important response to art. Here we have come to understand it interactively, as vital reciprocation, as central to the sharing that enables the pupil then to differentiate – as central, therefore, to publication.

In this conversation between Malcolm and Sally the vital dimension of praise is missing. This is simply the result of Malcolm's never having seen the dance in performance. He has had no direct access to the piece and can, as a result, offer Sally no ambience of public praise to support her self-appraisal. This does not mean that the conversation is entirely without benefit to her. On the contrary it demonstrates very clearly the potential of shared talking in the betwixt and between mode to re-awaken and revive an experience undergone and to clarify and order it as *conscious understanding* in reflection. However, it also serves to emphasize the essential role, in a completely satisfying conversation, of shared, direct engagement with the artwork in question. This particular conversation was one of the first attempts by the project team to explore what such a conversation might be like and occurred between phases 2 and 3 of the project. The conversation between Malcolm and Louise occurred some two months later (phase 3) and reflects an advance in our understanding.

Malcolm begins by asking Sally to describe what happened in the dance.

S: Well, what happened was it was set in a bedroom
which had twin beds – [points] one there and one
there – and here was a window, a rather fine window,
with curtains and shutters which we discovered at
some stage . . . and, um, we started from behind the   5
curtains and opened the shutters, um . . .

M: So effectively the room was dark?

S: The room was dark to start with.

M: Uhm.

S: And then the room became light when we opened   10
the shutters. We sat on the windowsill and then
opened the curtains so it became lighter and that's
when we were revealed. The funny thing about
working it out was that we had to be aware of the
effect that it was going to have.   15

M: So you were thinking of audience, weren't you?

S: Um . . . yes, we had to . . .

M: . . . in some sense.

S: . . . and in fact the course director was the one who made
us realize that because when we started off we were   20
less aware . . .

M: Yeah.

S: . . . of how we might be looking – and how we could
maximize the effect.

M: Just carry on telling me what you looked like and   25
what you did.

S: Um, so this was pretty much identical and we were
trying to follow a symmetry between us and then we
moved over on to the beds and we changed it a little
bit there so that we were doing similar things but in   30
quite different forms.

M: One moved to one bed, one to the other bed.

S: Yes. That's right. Um, and then we just went through
a process . . .

M: You sat down together?   35

S: Yes, we did sit down together but in different
positions and then we actually did different things for
a while, but complementary things.

M: What sort of things?

S: Um, we were exploring the surface of the bed and   40
the textures of it all made up.

M: How?

S: By touching it, smoothing it, looking at it. That kind of thing. Um, oh, I think I actually . . .

M: I can't see what you're dressed in.   45

S: Well, when we were doing it we were just dressed in our ordinary clothes – when we were rehearsing it – and eventually we were wearing our nighties which caused a lot of giggles. Um, in fact, yes, there was a light at the head of my bed so I used that. I went   50 across and switched it on.

M: So the impression that I'm getting is that of two women in a bedroom preparing to go to bed.

S: That's right.

Although she can give him no more than her 'insider' view, Sally can quite successfully recall and describe her dance for Malcolm. She succeeds in making Malcolm 'see' her dance as *she* saw it, though he can offer her no 'seeing' of his own. The question of how to talk about performance art has often been raised for us by the teachers we have consulted: how do you focus on a piece that is not tangibly present, that has apparently disappeared into thin air? One solution has been to use a video or audio recording but this is not satisfactory. It distorts the real issue by supplying the perspective of the audience (and a distorted version of it) as definitive, thus marginalizing the performer's 'insider' perception. Not having seen Sally's dance, Malcolm does the next best thing, which is to glean sufficient information to enable him to realize the performance *imaginatively*; he works hard to understand Sally's perspective. Ideally 'insider' and 'outsider' perceptions should inform, modify and support one another.

Malcolm invites Sally to move on to consider the 'depth' dimension of the piece.

M: There is imagery here . . . there is an image, there are   55 images . . . um, with evocative associations. Were you aware of possible associations? Were you aware at all that there might be . . . you know, of feelings and of ideas that went beyond simply the pattern of pleasing movements?

S: Yeah, I think we . . .   60

M: What were they? And are you prepared to talk about them?

S: [Laughs.] We had to be a bit aware of that. I think that when Liz and I were actually doing it we did enter into this sort of 'play' a lot and we could be content with that but it's the audience that made the difference, um, because suddenly there we were.   65

M: And the prospect of an audience.

S: Two young women in the bedroom.

M: Yeah.   70

S: And, I mean, you can't divorce the fact that these are beds and there we are in our nighties and everything from the sexual and sensual side of it. So you had – the audience forced us to be aware of us as sort of looked at and . . .   75

M: OK, let's stop a minute. You're saying that that was the prospect of and in the end the actual event of an audience.

S: Yeah.

M: Now, that's in a sense saying that *all* that is . . . all those connotations . . . you use the words 'sexual', 'sensual' . . . those only entered into *your* perception of what was going on because you had a feeling that somebody was going to be watching. Is that true?   80

S: Um . . . Well, I'd say that we were . . .   85

M: Was it not part of what you were actually doing?

S: I'd say that we were probably aware of it at the time and certainly . . .

M: Did you not explore that as well?

S: Not consciously. We explored the sensual side of it but not the sexual side . . .   90

M: Touching all the sheets and the . . .

S: Yes, and we may have giggled occasionally which may have . . .

M: Indicated what?   95

S: That we did realize, y'know, that this was quite an intimate and maybe sort of like provocative sort of thing to be doing.

M: Uhm.

S: Um, but we were [laughs] more from the sensual side because it didn't seem threatening. It was play. Um [pause] . . . and we must have . . . yes, I suppose we   100

must have been aware of that. Um [pause] . . . but
[pause] . . . but that – yes, OK, it was there – but the
nature of it changed once the audience were there   105
and once we had reaction from the audience.

M: It seems to me that the whole thing about the
performance and the audience is – it feels to me as if
that actually is a massive factor.

S: I think it was.   110

Very early on in the conversation the issues of subjectivity and
objectivity, privacy and exposure, are identified as being of major
significance. These are key feelings for several reasons. The two
dancers are inexperienced and quite naturally feel inhibited as
composers and performers. The theme 'going to bed' is, again, a
potentially sensitive area on account of the association with private
behaviours – intensified by considerations of dressing and undress-
ing, retiring and attiring for the night. The situation, the nature and
the parameters of the task set by the course director aroused contrary feelings of anxiety and excitement which come to dominate
the practical and the expressive dimensions of the making process
for both the participants. As the improvisation suggests possibilities
the piece develops its own character. Sally makes clear that although
she is aware all the time of the need to consider the way the dance
will look to a possible viewer she expects to find and does find
the act of performing – of becoming what she calls 'the object of
somebody's gaze' – troubling. The issue of audience remains 'a
massive factor' for her, arguably because Malcolm cannot make
that audience (the 'other' viewpoint) known to her, he cannot
reassure her or resolve it for her. At the end of the conversation she
still does not know what impression she made upon the audience
and this makes self-assessment very difficult.

The sense of uncertainty is compounded by the fact that –
as becomes clear towards the end of the second part of the
conversation – Sally didn't feel entirely in control of her material:

S: I didn't feel I was in control of any overall feelings
about the thing. And that's what I would like to have had.

Sally wanted to be able to sense the piece 'as a whole'. She felt
she was 'like an instrument of the dance', subject to 'the situation we were in, the task we'd been set.' She senses that the act of

transformation was incomplete. She experienced difficulty in 'seeing' the piece as something to look at while composing it as something to move or be within.

> S: I think there was a kind of discrepancy between the
>   doing of it . . . and this external thing that it was.

Sally was able, in collaboration with her partner, to explore the way gesture works as an expressive medium, and to begin to transform some quite difficult and ambiguous feelings into forms she found both pleasing and significant. She recalls the *mis-en-scène* – the physical aspects of the room and its furnishings – in vivid detail and tells the 'story' of the dance in an assured and graphic manner. She appears to have forgotten nothing. Asked to convey the key movement of the dance (its 'holding form') she has no problem – it is a gesture that goes with the idea of 'revealing'. She speaks of 'a movement to do with the hand . . . a pushing away movement, a kind of drawing back.' There are many interwoven themes – in particular the contrast between submission and admission and between solemnity and play. These express the tension between, on the one hand, being controlled by the form and, on the other, behaving naturally within the form: a dialectic of ritual and routine. This was felt as an important ambiguity in the eventual content of the dance.

> M: Were you aware of any particular form-making in   120
>   yourself that you found pleasurable or interesting,
>   where you thought, 'I liked doing that. I liked that
>   movement'?
> S: Um . . . yes, I s'pose so. I suppose that's why I pick on
>   the kind of pushing away movement, pushing against   125
>   something which – I mean, I'm thinking of, say, the
>   curtain that was running down and it was a turning
>   from looking out across the garden, stretching the
>   hand out [turns head to left; sweeps right arm across
>   her body from low on the left side high into the air   130
>   on the right] and not looking at the curtain but
>   knowing it was there because that's where it had
>   been left and [sweeps right arm backwards as if
>   drawing a large curtain] pushing it back that way . . .
>   [inaudible] . . . and then the rest of the body following 135

round, the eyes coming round to see what had been
done. And following that through as a kind of pivot
with your hand there [on the curtain], to bring the
whole of the rest of the body to stand up [head, eyes
and left hand move smoothly round to the right] and   140
to pull the curtain down with force to pull it back.

M: Right. So . . .

S: And that was something which seemed to have some
coherence to it, a flow, which went right the way
through, which not all of the gestures that we worked   145
out did . . . they were more . . . smaller, not followed
through.

M: Right, but you were aware that that gesture, as you
call it, did occur again, that it was there, or aspects of
it were elsewhere in what you did.   150

S: Yes . . . and we did try to think in terms of sequences
through different time . . . [inaudible] . . . through different
parts of our body. Pushing from your waist and so
on were bits we did subsequently.

M: Did you talk about that? Did you say 'Let's . . .'?   155

S: Yes, I think we must have done because it was to do
with facing that way and then 'Let's face this way
and twist here.'

M: Uhm.

S: Probably as well, that particular gesture came quite   160
early on in our doing of it and sort of gave us the
confidence to and a sort of theme to follow through.
We knew what we were doing because we felt it was
right.

The sensuality of the occasion is expressed through gestures of
stroking and pressing, unfolding and pulling back, of abandon and
demureness. Sally explains the attraction that she feels to the
elements of the bedding itself, the pillows (to be punched), eider-
down (bouncy, puffy), the covers (to be thrown off), the fine cotton
sheets (to be smoothed). She discovers characteristic sounds (thud-
dings). There are, in the course of shared exploration, important
insights for her about dance as an expressive medium – acquired
in part from working with the director in preparation for the making
of the piece.

S: We had been trained in this way of looking at things   165
   . . . It's looking with your body rather than just with
   your eyes.

She goes on to explain what she means:

S: Well, say you were looking at a bedspread, and it's
   got these little textures on it, it's not just sort of looking
   at it and . . . um . . . recognizing it to yourself but   170
   somehow showing that looking in your touching and
   in the way that you'll approach the thing, in the way
   that you might move towards it. So it's making
   something manifest. . . .

Sally explains that the process of exploration, of play in the
medium, with the physical materials that evoked and supported the
gestures and movements, was 'very like contemplating the whole
thing'. The challenge of the dance itself was 'to do with filling up
space' in the sense of 'bringing this space to life'.

S: The space isn't really registered as a space until its   175
   boundaries have been defined in some way. I mean,
   it's just a room that we were in. And to make everyone
   watching . . . um . . . it had to be visibly shown to them.
M: The space? You mean the space?
S: Yes, and . . .   180
M: The space had to be articulated in some way, by,
   through the moves that you were making?
S: Yes, and brought to attention, through *our* attention
   to it.
M: Right, yes – and to the materials that are in the space? 185
S: Yes, that would be part of the space – I mean the
   forms that the furniture and things make in the air
   there . . .

An interesting recurring theme in the conversation – one that
becomes crucial in the end to Sally's reservations about the dance
itself – is the distinction and tension between the formal elements
(gestures, movements) and the sense of potential 'deeper' meanings
that perhaps called for more dramatic treatment. Sally is aware
of the relational and dramatic possibilities in the situation: two
women preparing for bed. They were aware 'that this was quite an

intimate and maybe sort of like provocative sort of things to be doing,' but concentrating upon the sensual side 'didn't seem threatening'. Later in the conversation Sally suggests that 'eye contact', actually avoided in the dance, would have added an entirely extra element – but 'I don't think we felt confident enough about that.' She goes on to see this omission from the work as a possible flaw, detracting from the energy, coherence and 'reasoning' (as she calls it) behind the dance. She says at the end of the conversation that she would like to continue working on the piece and that this additional 'surface' material would be the thing she would want to try to address.

> S: I would like to, having thought about it and edged
> towards the issues. I mean, I haven't actually   190
> thought about it beforehand, but having edged
> towards the issues and thought what they are, it
> would be interesting to explore them and see how –
> what were the missing avenues . . . and to see what
> could be put together in a way that would be righter,   195
> more right.

Summary

The conversation permits Sally to 'edge' towards conscious insights that would allow her to continue the work prompted by the project and that might eventually grant her full ownership of the piece. Given the considerable intrinsic challenge of the project and her own inexperience there were many problems and issues to be explored. Recalling what had been at once an enjoyable and a disturbing experience many weeks after the event proved to be a surprisingly constructive and satisfying experience. Malcolm pushed Sally to recollect concrete details and to struggle for insights that emerge slowly but inevitably during the course of the discussion, There is no sense of hurry; there is a generally relaxed tone and a readiness by both partners to be open, honest and particular.

Sally's aesthetic response

Appropriation

There is a good deal of concern with the nature of dance itself and the way gesture and movement catch and convey meaning. The course director had worked with the idea of movement that expressed seeing. Sally is aware of experiencing making and performing very differently, and of the effort required to face an audience. Skills are being sought and the effect of their absence appraised and contended with. Feeling, however, remains diffuse and never crystallizes as drive or desire.

Transformation

A strong sense of reciprocal engagement between feeling and form emerges during the discussion. The dance utilizes movement, physical objects and materials and sounds to create its sensate surface. Ambivalent feelings find expression in contradictory structures – the setting is used to amplify and extend the tensions between reticence and provocation, lassitude and arousal, ritual and routine discovered and embodied in significant movement. Transformation remains incomplete, however, to the extent that Sally felt the narrative and dramatic aspects of the dance were not properly explored. The patterning of movement and gesture achieved the effect of echo and reflection rather than connection, intimation between the two protagonists. Her sense of ownership was impaired.

Publication

This conversation provides a rather special instance of publication and – although the conversation was in a number of ways enjoyable and productive for both partners – it does serve to underline the crucial importance of *direct engagement* by both the participants with the 'present' art work. In this case, the fact that Malcolm had not actually experienced the dance meant that he could not offer Sally the all-important 'second-opinion' – he could not be the 'good enough other' whose function it is to receive, praise and validate the thing made from a point of vantage outside the expressive act. Sally is subjected to a rigorous examination that, for all Malcolm's clear interest in both the work and her, lacks the crucial element of shared perception, shared imagination, shared emotion. He can offer no fantasies of his own to encourage her to extend or rework hers. He cannot re-awaken the work in his own imagination since he has no memories of it. Above all the affective dimension is absent from publication here – that dimension that belongs to and is constitutive of 'praise'. Despite this serious handicap, the consequence of which is to leave Sally isolated and exposed (Malcolm can offer no 'cover'), she manages to survive and to emerge with an assurance and a set of descriminations that leave her ready and motivated to take up the work again and push on with it. A great deal of the sense and satisfaction that result from the conversation is directly attributable to Sally's power and confidence with words and her readiness to take most of the responsibility for publication with the minimum of support.

Conventionalization
Here again the conversation could not be particularly helpful, in as much as Malcolm could not speak for any audience. On the other hand, Sally's rich, assured account of her experience, particularly as maker if not as performer, indicates a strong sense of confidence in the authenticity and integrity of her aesthetic responses even if she remained uncertain about her powers of persuasion and control of her audience. The conversation works in a limited formative sense with Sally making all the running. Although the conversation offers little help to Sally in establishing her as a valid choreographer or dancer in her own eyes, it does succeed in bringing into conscious focus some of the key elements in her form-feeling encounter and in developing a practical strategy for the future.

Now entertain conjecture: further thoughts on
publication and conventionalization

The positive aspects of subjectivity in the processes of publication do not perhaps generally receive sufficient acknowledgement or emphasis. We are over-concerned with objectivity and critical detachment and miss occasions of enlightenment and understanding by disparaging engagement and surrender. The notions of 'praise', of the 'privileged' audience, of the 'potential' space, are all highly relevant to a complete understanding of this area. Publication invariably makes special demands not just of the one to be published but also of the public that receives it. We are suggesting that artists (and children as artists) should not shy away from talking about their work or from using talk to explore their work creatively with their audience (including their teacher as audience). But we now want to look again at the role of the 'receiver' a little more closely.

In her essay, 'How should one read a book?' (1933), Virginia Woolf advises the receiver of a written text:

> Do not dictate to your author; try to become him. Be his fellow-worker and accomplice. If you hang back, and reserve and criticise at first, you are preventing yourself from getting the fullest possible value from what you read. But if you open your mind as widely as possible, then signs and hints of almost imperceptible fineness from the twist and turn of the first sentences, will bring you into the presence of a human being unlike any other.
>
> (in Woolf 1966: 2)

Such a positive, believing (rather than sceptical) attitude is the receiver's vital contribution to the process of publication, whether the privileged 'first receiver' is the parent or teacher or friend, or a remoter public. It is incumbent upon her, him or them to reward integrity, authenticity, courage and commitment, 'to receive impressions with the utmost understanding' (Woolf 1966: 8) – even where they might feel personally disappointed in terms of the emotional or imaginative impact of the work.

The act of sympathy and engagement is not the end of the receiver's role: in-dwelling is followed by reflective judgement, but decidedly in that order, as a process of completion wherein lies satisfaction (see comments made in Chapter 5).

If publication involves some of the notions suggested here it is important to approach it in the educational context with rather more care and consideration than is customary. Praise, for example, should not be 'faint'; everyone knows what faint praise does. On the other hand, praise, for all its tendency towards admiration (Latin *mirare* = wonder) can also perfectly well accommodate criticism, provided it is, and is felt to be, constructive. Praise, to do its work, must be full-blooded, and it must be informed. Praise is an acknowledgement, a re-cognition, an admission, an expression of belief: *credo*. What we are after is an account of ap-praisal which does not imply a rejection of or a rebuke to the artist, the maker, the pilgrim (as a person) – the soul seeking after truth and beauty.

In formative assessment the teacher must remain faithful to the principles of devotion and dedication: to both the artist and, of course, to art. The teacher as guardian looks both ways. Where devotion and dedication break down or are forfeited then the whole enterprise founders since the relationship of mutual esteem upon which it absolutely depends has been lost. Even with more disinterested publics, something of the same obtains. There need be no contradiction, no breach of trust, when summative assessments are made, if self-assessment and other-assessment have, by that time, been allowed to coincide. The research conversations confirm this.

All artists and makers confront a public. Sometimes the business is to make a financial transaction; sometimes a social or convivial one; on other occasions the transaction is semantic – the making of meaning together, e.g. between performer and audience. In a sense every artist's first, most immediate public is herself. Both during the making process and afterwards she tries to adopt an objective perspective, she tries imaginatively to stand outside the formative act and place the work in the public arena as she knows it to be in her own experience and as she understands it in the experience of others. Where artists work in groups or with partners they can act in this capacity for each other. However, in so far as they are all implicated in the creative work, they may find it difficult and strange to stand outside, and impossible to divest themselves entirely of their subjective investment. After all, when the artist stands back to check what she has done against what she feels, against what she wishes or desires to see, in espousing a measure of objectivity, it must not be at the expense of subjectivity. And when she is being objective hers is not at all the real perspective of the genuine outsider – the work still demands external validation. Publication is manifested as 'the public'.

A similar relationship to audience obtains for the controller of a performance (theatre director, choreographer, orchestral conductor) or an artist working in the media (TV producer, film-maker, recording artist). For all these different makers the public exists 'outside', out there. They may all seek contact with an intermediary, with someone committed to supporting the making process one way or another through offering an 'interested' outsider perspective. But every artist probably needs the love of strangers. It is a high risk situation. She can either choose to remain passive and silent, or she can adopt a more interventionist role. Part of the

machinery of contemporary arts marketing has lent a new dimension to public relations in the arts, and artists nowadays are much
less reluctant than they used to be to discuss and promote their
work, i.e. to publicize it by talking about it. It must be clear by now
that the project, too, sees real value in public talk – as a crucial
aspect of creative arts teaching and learning. The problem is that we
don't know very much about this kind of talk and are not (yet)
very good at it.

In the performing arts the situation is significantly more
complex – certainly so when we mean 'live' performance. We
recognise the possibility – even the necessity – of a special dimension in experience arising from the co-presence of audience and
performer in the same place at the same time. A great performance
cannot happen except in the presence of and with the participation
of a 'great' audience. The quality of the audience is as critical in
determining the quality of a performance as the quality of the
material and of the performer(s). Performers seek to perform not
simply for or even to their audience, but with them. Audiences are
required to make themselves available, to become present as a
living, responsive milieu for the performer – they are required to
enter into the event reciprocally with the performer, to 'suffer', to
bear witness, to keep watch, to be com-passionate, to offer their
silence to her sound, their stillness to her movement, their darkness
to her light. Herein the good audience corresponds closely to our
conception of the good conversationist – the good listener, good
looker. We have to understand listening, looking and suffering as
constructive, constitutive, creative responses. A live performance is
a collaborative undertaking. We lend her our eyes and ears, but
much more than that: we are in some vital, critical sense instrumental to her performance. Our compassionate attention releases her
performance, secures and channels it. We are a living dimension
of her inspiration, her breath of life. Without us she suffocates,
collapses under the burden of the inert weight of the piece
unimagined. We speed her. She needs our palpable presence if she
is truly to be there for us. For our part we demand her total sacrifice,
her surrender of herself to our creative imagining, to our passionate
listening and looking, to our desire for her truth, her beauty (which
is our only way to dream the true and beautiful).

Audience and performer meet each other as question and answer.
In arts education we don't do enough to educate children in

audiencing – as living, contemplative, compassionate witnesses upon whose imaginations the artist plays, and whose hands and voices, whose praise (applause) alone can break the spell and release her.

There are performers. There are also composers who perform what they have composed and there are performers who compose as they perform (improvise a performance). For these last two types of performer the personal strains and demands are obviously compounded. The public performance becomes the arena in which they find themselves on trial on several counts simultaneously. Shakespeare understood these strains well and refers to them frequently in his work. He also understood the special relationship between performer and audience. Audiences must be able to use their imaginations. Certainly the teacher talking with her pupils in the kind of way that we have been exploring cannot escape the demand to be present imaginatively.

> Now entertain conjecture of a time
> When creeping murmur and the poring dark
> Fills the wide vessel of the universe . . .
> (King Henry V, Act IV, Prologue)

To attend, to witness, to wait, to suffer, above all to attend as audience is precisely to 'entertain conjecture'. Shakespeare, in the same speech, bids us 'sit and see; Minding true things by what their mockeries be.' The teacher, partnering her or his pupils, 'minding true things' and with only 'mockeries' to go by, faces just such a summons: to entertain conjecture, to inhabit possible worlds of feeling, now. 'Gently to hear, kindly to judge.'

Case study 7: Talking Picture

Malcolm and Jack

In this conversation, Jack, an 11 year old, talks about his 'home' painting of a Cornish cliff scene which he did on holiday some months before the conversation. Jack is Malcolm's son. The conversation begins with his remembering the place and the difficulties he had in drawing it since the tide was going out at the time, thereby revealing more and more of the rocks. The technical difficulties are

Talking Picture

not dwelt upon. Rather, Malcolm seeks first to uncover Jack's interest in the content of the picture. This is the uncovering of feeling, attraction, curiosity, desire, rather than of productive process.

M: And what made you choose this particular bit [of cliff]
    to look at?
J: Um, it was a nice part and, uh, also . . . this . . . was . . . um . . .
    this had a certain amount of expression in the face of
    the rock. There was all sorts of colours and shapes   5
    and it was quite jagged – the face of the rock.
M: What, what . . . was it that attracted you to it? I mean,
    what made you choose this bit of the rock to look at?
    I mean, on the picture [pointing to it] it looks as if we
    are looking at an inlet, where the water comes in –   10
    almost into a little kind of cove or something like that.
J: Yeah. Well, what attracted me about this was . . . it was
    sort of a rough and rugged place. I like places like that.
M: When you did it can you remember having a clear
    idea what the picture was going to turn out like?   15
J: Not really. I . . . I had a rough idea but all those ideas
    basically changed when I was drawing it . . . Um . . . uh,
    I . . . I thought that I was going to draw the little sort of
    town that was on top of these cliffs. Um, but then I
    decided to only draw a couple of houses.   20

Jack first asserts his liking for the place itself – that particular piece of coastline. He does so again at line 13. He talks from memory, recalling the *sensate elements* of the scene: colour, shape, texture. There is an interesting if unconscious resonance in Jack's notion that the *face* of the rock has what he calls 'expression', suggesting immediate sensate engagement beyond the surface level. Jack talks about his liking for 'rough and rugged places' – this place was not simply momentarily interesting to him, it was already at home within an existing system of desire and significance. This somehow strengthens the reasons for painting, helps him to form and build the painting in response to inner impulse rather than simply to work at a faithful reproduction. This sense of impulse is confirmed as the conversation progresses and the model – the actual landscape – is relinquished and the painting becomes suffused with a personal and particular mood. Lines 16–20 show evidence of this development from neutral perception to active selection.

It is of no concern to Jack that his picture does not accurately depict the scene he was looking at. Jack knows (conventionalization) that pictures can have value in themselves, can dictate their own terms. His confidence anticipates the degree of authority, authenticity and ownership that becomes increasingly evident as the conversation progresses.

In the next extract Malcolm seems to be encouraging Jack to focus his perception through an appeal to his own subjective experiencing of the work. The question (early in the conversation) is an open one, leaving the criteria for 'liking best' to be chosen by Jack himself.

M: If we look at the picture, what bits of the picture do
    you feel happiest with, do you like best?

J: Um . . . I like these bits down at the bottom, where you
    can see the water and the rocks, and there's dark
    shadows in the water. Um . . . and I like it where, here   25
    where there's . . . um, like it's a sheer drop, it's straight
    down . . . and you can actually see that [points to a
    'stack' of rock rising sheer out of the water]. And
    usually I'm not very good at drawing those things.
    . . . Uh . . . I also like this bit up here where . . . um [He   30
    points up to the left-hand side of the picture. He was
    originally pointing down to the bottom right. He's
    pointing up now to the middle left where there
    is a high cliff face.] . . . where there is a contrast between
    the jagged rocks and the grass and the earth and the   35
    shrubs up at the top, which are on . . . like the hill.

M: Is it the feel of it or, or the colours you've got, or, or
    the shapes of it, or, or because you really feel
    you've caught, you know, that . . . that contrast?

J: I feel I've caught that contrast, yeah, between . . . the   40
    . . . browny nice greeny, browny earthy colour and the
    grey . . . rock face.

Jack's response (23–36) is full and varied. He points out areas in the picture, distinguishing one element from another. In lines 26–27 – 'like it's a sheer drop, it's straight down . . . and you can actually see that' – he communicates the sense and the quality of what he sees with authority, at the same time offering it to Malcolm to share (publication). His perceptual satisfaction is endorsed by the reflection (29) that this is also a technical achievement. The poise and freedom of this speech is further indication of what we have come to mean by publication. Jack's attention moves across the picture, exploring and simultaneously revealing it through the medium of conversational talk. The movement of his gaze, from bottom to top, left to right, itself creates the dimensions of the picture. These can be included in the sensate constructs he generates. At lines 34–36 he indicates that he sees the individual elements in contrastive relations – he is beginning to order the piece, to discern its structure, its formal character. Malcolm's subsequent question registers a living interest in what he has just heard. He appears a little unsure of what he wants to ask, hesitantly moving towards an interpretation and at the same time seeking further clarification, easing Jack a little deeper, but not too quickly.

M: Um, what would you say was the mood of this
   picture? Would you say it had a mood, a feeling
   about it?   45
J: Um, yeah, it's . . . It looks like it might be a wet, dreary,
   rainy day that could, you know, it looks a bit blowy . . .
   Um . . . uh . . . you could imagine . . . that there was . . . a
   bit of a storm and the storm had passed and it was after
   the storm a bit.   50
M: So what sort of mood is that?
J: Uh . . . well, again it's a . . . um . . . it's like a rough,
   rainy day, not really angry. It's not really angry . . . um . . .
   just, uh . . . it's not bad. It's a nice mood. It's not happy
   like in the summer, but my feelings, um, you know,   55
   feelings don't have to be happy in the summer and
   unhappy in the winter, because I like this feel and I
   drew this not quite how it looked at the time but
   how I wanted it to look.
M: You are saying there are contrasting qualities in the   60
   picture, contrasting moods. You're saying . . . I'd like
   you to explore a little bit more the idea that the
   storm has passed, that the angry feeling has passed.
   Yet it's still around, isn't it? There are memories of
   it somehow or other. It's, it's not long since the storm   65
   has passed, is that right?

J: Yeah. Um . . . um . . . it's like the storm had been overnight
     and it's calming down in the . . . uh, morning.
M: Uhm [agreeing] . . . There's still a kind of sadness about
     it somehow?   70
J: Yeah . . . um . . .
M: Did you say 'sad'? I don't know whether that was a
     word you used. Something like that after angry and . . .
J: Yeah, well, it's not really sad, um . . . it's . . . dull . . . a bit,
     and . . .   75
M: That was the mood you wanted to catch.
J: Yeah.

Jack takes an active interest in the surface of the picture: the way
shapes and colours work together and the way certain aspects
of the content are depicted. Here Malcolm encourages him to
consider its affective qualities. Jack gives an interpretative response.
The 'wet, dreary, rainy day' (46–47) is not actually depicted
(denoted) in the picture but it is evoked (connoted) through it, in a
curiously concrete way. It is not a question of *seeing* but of *feeling*
the rain, the dreariness, the wind. These feelings are tentatively
evoked, couched in the conditional tense, the result of present
(recent) looking and open to revision: 'It looks like it might be . . .',
'You could imagine . . .' (46–48). This last 'You could imagine'
introduces a context to the piece – the passing of a storm. The
mention of the storm gives the the picture a complexity, a hint
perhaps of *mixed feelings*. And at the same time it manages the
complexity by arranging it as a sequential narrative (i.e. meaningful)
structure.[3] Malcolm presses him to synthesize his account to say
what it means in the 'now' of the picture: 'What sort of mood
is that?'

Jack begins again to consider, feeling around among possible
words for ones that might be good enough for his expressive purpose
here. He develops from the concrete images suggestive of mood
('rough, rainy') towards the more abstract emotional attribute
'angry'. He finds he cannot specify the mood of the painting exactly,
but approximates through negatives. Because the scene is 'not really
angry', 'not bad', it takes on overtones of anger and badness, at
the same time evading and exceeding these. His is a vital, fluid use
of language in an attempt at emotional particularity.

To explain what he means he offers an organized ratiocinative statement that contrasts general assumptions ('happy like in the summer') with his personal experiencing ('feelings don't have to be happy in the summer'): it is through subjective perception that the objective scene comes to be evocative. He uses summer and winter as polarized instances, a popular oppositional construct, to make a sophisticated case for the transformative power and validity of his own feelings. Because of its argumentative structure, his assertion of authenticity is also a persuasion – both stating and making a point. This is an instance of confident authenticity – the sentence itself a conventionalizing operation.

His statement is concluded and confirmed by the actual occasion: 'because I like this feel and I drew this not quite how it looked at the time but how I wanted it to look' (57–59). Analysis of the sensate constructs here would oppose 'rough and rainy' to 'summer', but at the same time align them to 'summery feelings' (fusion). The summer–winter construct takes on a form which is mutable when it comes into play with feeling. The two poles of the construct are related dialectically rather than simply contrasted – evidence of sophisticated sensate ordering.

In lines 60–66 Malcolm offers an interpretation of what he has heard, but also questions, wanting more. His words are not neutral but are searching and suggestive. He appears to be trying to sense as well as recall what Jack has been saying.

M: OK . . . um . . . what about the houses at the top right of the picture? Are they important in the picture?

J: Um, well . . . if I hadn't have drawn them it would have 80 been . . . you could have imagined this picture to have been like a . . . a place maybe near the sea where nobody's actually living there and nobody's been there or anything. And these houses, they're a bit . . . old houses really ... um ... uh ... there isn't people walking 85 around. I think that might spoil it if there were people walking around. And there's a little house down here [points down left]. It's probably, it's probably, I imagine that to be somewhere where some old man who had been very active before . . . and . . . was not 90 quite so active now, liked looking over into the sea and on to the cliffs.

M: So the houses are kind of signs of human beings,

of humanity, of human presence, in a way, but
there's no actual human beings. The houses are   95
just watching, just . . .

J: Yeah, um . . . there doesn't really have to be anyone
living in the houses necessarily. Um . . . uh . . .

M: There's a contrast there too, isn't there . . .

J: Yeah . . .   100

M: Between the houses and their feel for people, and
all this violent, rough, wild nature. Is that right? Is
that a kind of . . . ? And up here you've got a sense
of order, fields and roads, and the lines are straight,
and a sense of greenness and so on . . . [inaudible].   105

J: Yeah, well . . . up at the top it looks quite man-made
really . . . and down at the bottom, where the rocks are,
it's . . . unspoiled, and it's how I would like it to be
really. That's 'cause I like places like that – that are
unspoiled and rugged. At the top there's . . . as I said,   110
it's all straight lines and things like that. Man-made.

In this extract Malcolm opens a new way into the picture by selecting particular elements and questioning their significance.

Curiously Jack talks first about the picture as it would have been
without the houses, uninhabited, untouched. This sense pervades
the scene and characterizes the houses and their significance in the
picture. It is as if the force of the natural environment diminishes the
human influence, makes it vestigial. At lines 108–9 Jack describes
this as 'how I would like it to be really'. Without prompting, Jack
gives the scene an imagined narrative content in the form of an old
man, once active, now contemplative. A connection with storm and
calm is perhaps not too fanciful; here is the same underlying feeling
given different expression. The old man's house is actually located at
the cliff top, i.e. at the point where the man-made and the natural
meet. Again the ambivalent, dialectical idea – shown in the calm
activity vestigial in retirement, the past in the present – is strung out
in the time and space structure offered by narrative. The narrative
seems to act as a rudimentary device for grasping the whole in
the process of talk, the gestalt of the picture.

Again Malcolm's response is full and interpretive both of what
Jack has been saying and of what he himself perceives. By line 99
he offers his own perception of contrast, licensed by the openings

Jack has provided, and Jack accepts and develops his idea, using it as a basis to reiterate his preference for the 'unspoiled and rugged' (110) as if the contrast affirms this.

M: Uh, I feel this is a very bold picture. It's got a
tremendous energy in it and it's very free. Um, the
lines are wonderfully strong and very . . . and the
whole picture is very 'large'. I mean, the way you   115
have handled everything is on a very . . . is somehow
or other bold and strong and free. I don't feel that
you've been crabbed or . . . inhibited or enclosed by
what you are doing. You've really, you've looked at
it and you've taken it and it's a very, very bold and rich   120
and . . . and terrifically vigorous painting, picture. Do
you see what I'm saying?

J: Yeah, and I agree with you 'cause that's how I
painted it, drew it – it's bold and I put lots of colour
on. Where . . . up the top where the grass is, there's   125
lots of browns and greens . . .

M: Is the colour important in this picture?

J: Yeah, I think so . . . When I drew it in pencil it did look
OK . . . but not as nice as this, not as good as it looks
now.   130

Malcolm goes on to give a very full and positive evaluation of the painting (112–122). The expansive language he uses to describe the picture is used again to convey his sense of how Jack handled the making; both are bold, strong and free. The 'tremendous energy' of the painting is conflated with the sense that its painter has not 'been crabbed or inhibited or enclosed' – the form is seen as expressive of feeling. Jack complies quite naturally with this assessment, understanding it not as a point of closure, but as a reason for returning to the picture. This is praise indeed!

M: Do you feel the picture all holds together?

J: Yeah, yeah . . . I think so. Um . . .

M: Can you point out how it all ties up? What does hold
it all together? Make it one thing.

J: Um . . . I think . . . all . . . er . . . the sea helps. And all . . . 135

M: What does the sea do?

J: It . . . er . . . well, it keeps it all one thing. If you see it

like I do, the sea is a link between all of the other parts
because it's touching all of them . . . and the rocks
might grow out of the sea . . . Up here where the rocks   140
and the green-brown grass join, you can see where
the round shapes are, where it goes along the top.
And this part here, you could say that looks like . . . er
. . . like that cliff face might not be joined on to anything
but up the top you can see quite clearly that there is   145
a joining part. It's a bit like a silhouette drawing of
somebody's face. You can see all the outline but . . .
er . . . the nose doesn't have to be, you know, isn't on
the other side joined on to anything. It doesn't have to
be solid.   150

Malcolm's role is to help Jack to focus. At lines 133–134 he asks
him to venture a solution to the puzzle of how the picture holds
together. Malcolm's request that he 'make it one thing' is like a
playful exercise, an experiment with looking: 'given these rules,
what can you find out?' It is also a very important move in exploring
aesthetic understanding – Jack's sense of his painting as an
'inviolable whole' (Langer 1953). For Jack wholeness is at one and
the same time a formal, an emotional and an imaginative matter.

Again Jack is confident in publication, inviting Malcolm to share
his way of ordering the picture: 'If you see it like I do . . .'. He
speculates freely and allows his attention to move from the sea to the
rocks that 'grow' out of it up to where the rocks meet the earth. Now
he is talking quite abstractly about the shapes, so that he entertains
the perceptual possibility that the cliff face may be free-standing.
This is of interest to him rather than a matter of concern. He
associates the illusory and ambiguous effect with a silhouette
drawing – an acute comparison which suggests an understanding
of how the mind supplies information to complete and make sense
of what the eyes see. Jack is very willing for this piece to be open in
this way to the play of the senses and of meaning, both his own
and Malcolm's.

Malcolm then proceeds to play a 'projective' game with Jack
and his picture. (Compare Malcolm's similar move towards the
end of his conversation with Louise in case study 5.) He invites Jack
to select some of the different representational elements in the
picture, i.e. aspects of its surface (e.g. the sea, the old man's house,

the sky, the cliff face), and then to interpret them by imagining himself as each of them in turn, saying how that feels. For instance:

M: What about this house [top right]? Could you be this house or not? And is this house a man or a woman?

J: I think this house is a woman, because . . . it looks like it could be female.

M: What does she say sitting up there? 155

J: [in a tiny, high voice] 'I'm just sitting on the hill here and trying to keep all tidy but it's quite difficult with all these, all these storms playing around me, and I really don't know where I am. The smoke from my fire is being blown all over my face and I don't know what's 160 happening. I feel quite dizzy . . .'.

Later he decided that the rock face was also female and adopting 'her' voice, he said:

J: 'I feel . . . I'm a bit tired at the moment and . . . the sea has been splashing against me and wearing some of my skin off during the past years, and the storm just now was quite vicious and violent and I don't 165 feel well at all. I feel quite sick.'

This was an exercise in imaginative presentness. Finally Malcolm sums up:

M: So in your picture there are a whole lot of feelings – your feelings. There are strong feelings of the storm and of the storm having passed, and of danger and of anger and of all sorts of strange . . . Many sorts of 170 contrasting feelings, but overall the feel of the painting is that things have calmed down and come together and the sea is somehow connecting everything in this new calm – even if it's cold and the day is dull. Um . . . is that sort of right? 175

J: Yeah.

The conversation is concluded. Jack says:

J: It was interesting and I enjoyed being the different parts of my picture. Um . . . I understand it more than I did when I was drawing it.

M: Do you still like it as much?   180
J: Yeah I do . . . er . . . I specially like the rocks up here more.
M: Show me.
J: [pointing] Up round here.
M: The area we've just been talking about: the area that
      is female and was wounded and made sick by the   185
      storm?
J: Yeah.
M: It's almost as if you've just discovered that really.
J: Yeah . . . I didn't think about this picture this way at all
      when I was drawing it.   190

Talking is something else. Jack's satisfaction is very strong –
this exercise in publication has allowed him to re-experience his
drawing in a rich, lively and challenging way. This sharing with a
sympathetic (and delighting) companion has allowed Jack another
fruitful engagement with his feelings and left him calm, happy
and possibly wiser. Some moments after the conversation was
officially over, he began to comment further, now in a more
reflective mood. We are clearly in the final, judgemental phase:

J: Up here where the houses and roads are I think I
      could have done it a bit better . . . I didn't do it as
      carefully as I did all the others. I was in a hurry
      because I thought I might have to pack up soon . . . I
      might have got the proportions slightly wrong. Um . . .   195
      I still like that part . . .

Here the tape ran out.
What these case studies demonstrate in their different ways is
that involvement in arts activities – of many kinds and at many
levels – can generate dynamic, engaging, creative talk, which is
the grounds not for closure but for new discoveries, new learning.
This is an exciting revelation – one which we hope will motivate
the reader to adapt existing practices, to try new styles, new
approaches in talking to pupils, with the aim not just of monitoring
technique or of checking out taught knowledge, nor perfunctorily
of evaluating product, but of celebrating arts work in all its particularity and immediacy.

5

CONCLUSION

To call this chapter a Conclusion is somewhat misleading. It *is* an end, the end of a narrative, the end of our particular project, but it is not, we hope, the end of the enquiry; rather perhaps the opening chapter to a further enquiry undertaken by the reader. It must be seen as an invitation to the reader to engage in reflective talk, and to do so self-critically, recording the conversations, analysing them, re-engaging, risking again and more gravely. We have come to think that it is through such 'action research' that the findings of our project might best be tested and developed. Our book is concluded in precisely the sense that it requires individual readers now to make the technique their own.

As a result, we do not at this stage feel ready to offer more than a tentative suggestion as to how a summative pupil assessment report might look, how we might order and categorize the wealth of material uncovered and offered in shared conversation (see pp 140–1). The options must be kept open. It would not do to close down further empirical investigation prematurely: much more work has to be done. Too often in education the procedure for *recording* assessment information distracts from proper regard for the quality and character of the evidence. It is in this area of *quality of evidence* that we believe this project has made real gains. In two important respects we feel it places the arts in positions of increased strength and coherence: curriculum transaction and assessment. Both suggest ways forward for the arts in education.

The project began as an enquiry into the assessment of artistic expression and creativity in schools. We immediately became aware of a range of problems associated with the practices we encountered – openly acknowledged by our teachers as variously unsatisfactory, and probably immutable aspects, of what they felt was required of them. They felt uneasy about the possibility of damaging a pupil's self-esteem and undermining self-confidence when being critical or awarding a low mark in respect of personal, creative work. They worried lest they imposed their own preferences and tastes upon their pupils. They felt uncertain about the criteria of aesthetic quality they were using, sensing that these were often in conflict with the pursuit of individuality and singularity – two concepts closely associated with notions of artistic production and aesthetic education in our culture. They were uncomfortable about applying normative standards in judging pupils' work, and about fostering notions of comparison and competition. Given the inscrutability of the processes of expression and creativity – our particular chosen province of enquiry – the project's teachers generally preferred to concentrate on the practical and technical dimensions of art production, often making a more or less explicit separation in their own minds between the conscious and unconscious, the material and imaginative dimensions of artistic experience.

Moving towards talk as a means of exploring pupils' creative processes and evaluating their sense of their own achievement arose as no more than a hunch for us, in the first place. We wondered whether such a 'natural' procedure might supply a vital element missing from the assessment process as we were encountering it, namely the pupils' commentary on their own practice. Although we did not, at the time, recognize the full implications of the approach we were adopting, a radical reformulation of the initial research question was underway. We were in effect no longer asking how teachers might give an acceptable account of pupils' subjective experience, exemplified in their arts practice, but rather how pupils might be brought into the assessment process as what Schön (1983) calls 'reflective practitioners' in their own right. What was to impress us as our investigation progressed was the capacity for reflection and for articulation evinced in the pupils' participation in the assessment conversation. The problems we had with this approach, amply revealed in some of the case studies we have just examined, are both predictable and easily accounted for. What came as a real surprise, was not only the readiness of the pupils to seize the opportunity to talk about their work presented by the conversation format, but also their considerable, latent capacity for exploring, explaining and evaluating their aesthetic experience through talk. Assessment in the arts ceases therefore to begin and end with the teacher's perceptions, judgements and statements and turns right around to restore the work to its maker, the pupil. And so a new role emerges for the teacher: to equip the students with the reflective skills to monitor and assess their own work.

We came to a recognition of the relevance of Schön's work to our study late in our research.[4] He provided us with an invaluable set of ideas for illuminating and articulating our data. Schön contrasts two accounts of professional practice. The traditional account he describes in terms of what he calls 'technical rationality'. The process and assumptions characteristic of this account of what it is to behave as a professional he summarizes thus:

> According to the tradition of technical rationality, the profes- sions mediate between science and society and translate scien- tific research into social progress. The model of professional knowledge as technical expertise, based on the application of science, underlies the traditional contract between the auto- nomous professional expert and his client, the traditional exchange relationship between practitioner and researcher, and the rather paradoxical incorporation of ostensibly auto- nomous professionals within the highly specialized structures of bureaucratic systems.
>
> (Schön 1983: 338)

Against this pervasive model Schön demonstrates how most profes- sionals display other very different skills: the ability to improvise, to think on their feet, to respond sensitively and intuitively to situa- tions that are unique, uncertain and unstable. In other words, there is a professionalism that reveals itself not in applying standard procedures to particular 'cases' exemplifying general conditions, but rather as the ability spontaneously to reinterpret their skills in the light of particular, unpredictable problems, often entailing some degree of reformulation of the problem with which they felt themselves to be initially presented. What Schön repeatedly claims is that such professionals respond like *artists* – their practice is literally an art rather than an applied science. He calls this kind of activity 'artful inquiry'. It is impossible to read his book in the present political circumstances prevailing in education without reflecting that the official trend would appear to enforce an even more rigid form of technical rationality upon teaching as a profession and upon schools as bureaucratic institutions in which children are bound to learn what teachers are instructed to teach. The English National Curriculum specifies detailed attainment targets and programmes of study for all subjects in the curriculum, while teachers are required to 'deliver' the curriculum in the most cost-effective way possible. Teachers will be seen increasingly as technical experts in the science of instruction, rather than, for example, as partners with their pupils in processes of collaborative enquiry. For Schön, what distinguishes the technical-rationalist professional from the professional-as-artist is the capacity the latter displays for what he calls 'conversation with the situation'. By this he means the reciprocal interaction between the practitioners (engineer, designer, teacher, therapist) and the situation which not only confronts them but entails them as participants. The 'conversation' is a kind of thinking about what you are doing while you are doing it: a capacity for reflective thought that runs alongside practice and enriches it. The secret of 'conversation with the situation' is to be able to hear and respond to 'situation talk-back' with a mixture of impulse and deliberation, intuition and rationality.

It must by now be clear that Schön's discussion complements our own enquiry and illuminates it at many points. Consider, for instance, his account of the different approaches adopted by the expert (the technical rationalist) on the one hand and the reflective practitioner on the other (Table 3).

Schön's work has important implications for both partners to the assessment conversation in the arts – for the way the teacher proceeds in fashioning the conversation, and for the pupil's own development of the skills of reflection as a vital dimension of her own practice as an artist. In particular we would wish to stress the value of reflection, in action that is contemplative rather than productive. While acknowledging the value of reflection that

Table 3 Schön's expert and reflective practitioner contrasted

Expert	*Reflective practitioner*
I am presumed to know, and must claim to do so, regardless of my own uncertainty.	I am presumed to know, but I am not the only one in the situation to have relevant and important knowledge. My uncertainties may be a source of learning for me and for them.
Keep my distance from the client, and hold on to the expert's role. Give the client a sense of my expertise, but convey a feeling of warmth and sympathy as a 'sweetener'.	Seek out connections to the client's thoughts and feelings. Allow his respect for my knowledge to emerge from his discovery of it in the situation.
Look for deference and status in the client's response to my professional persona.	Look for the sense of freedom and of real connection to the client, as a consequence of no longer needing to maintain a professional façade.

accompanies and informs production (kinds of formative assessment requiring varying degrees of detachment from making during an ongoing process of production), we have been brought to appreciate, in the course of this research, the singular and remarkable insights that become possible through the various activities subsumed under the heading of what we have called publication – especially in transactions of praise, celebration and judgement. As most of our case studies illustrate, pupils are capable of rich and sophisticated responses to and understandings of their own work and seem well able to develop these responses and understandings in collaboration with their conversation partner. This phase of creative and expressive production in the arts is, we believe, considerably under-represented in most schools' practice and yields a field of opportunity for aesthetic knowing as well as appraisal of enormous potential; but, we must hasten to add, only when conducted in the reflective mode, which means that many teachers will have to discard present practices based almost entirely upon the principle of technical rationality. It could be argued that arts teachers need to behave more like real artists and less like bureaucrats. School art, at its worst, is the art of the bureaucrat: neat, safe, predictable, orthodox and amenable to MoT type testing. School art adds up: the real thing rarely does.

Schön suggests that a professional profile entails providing a particular set of answers to the following general, 'constant' questions:

1 What is the 'stuff' of the professional transaction: characteristic media, language and repertoire?
2 What appreciative systems facilitate and authorize judgement-making in the field?
3 What 'overarching theory' informs and underpins practice?
4 What sense of 'role' frames the relationship between professional and client?

He argues that this framework, these 'constant' questions, reveal both the differences between branches of a profession and the common features that allow some professionals to cluster into families with shared interests, principles and objectives. There is a sense in which arts teachers, history teachers, PE and English teachers are all fellow professionals and distinct from other professionals working in the law or science or management (though some common features exist). Within the arts we are aware of differences – certainly in terms of the 'stuff' of professional transactions – between art teachers and drama teachers, dance teachers and English teachers, music teachers and media teachers. But many of us would want to insist that the arts share significant common features and might reasonably be organized and presented in schools as a cognate and cohesive field of learning, knowing and practice. In particular, all arts teachers might be expected to share appreciative systems, an overarching theory and a sense of role relative to their students.

Schön's framework helps to clarify and explain some of the difficulties encountered by the project. These arose particularly in respect of questions 2, 3 and 4. The team and the teachers were all pretty much agreed what was meant by the 'stuff' of music, of art, of dance and of drama, though, to be fair, where drama was concerned the continuing division between drama as 'learning medium' and drama as 'theatre studies' meant we found ourselves in difficulty in some of our schools. However, more serious problems arose in connection with Schön's other three questions. For instance we were not always clear what 'appreciative systems' teachers were using in making their professional judgements. One English teacher, for instance, felt seriously threatened by the personal content of a particular pupil's writing and found it easier to give an E grade on the grounds that the writing failed to conform to the criteria of GCSE English than to acknowledge its undoubted (albeit deviant) literary merits as autobiographical writing for which it might well have received an A grade. More typically teachers applied normative technical-rational criteria in respect of technique and convention, and tended to ignore stylistic and aesthetic considerations (appropriation and transformation). We have tried to show that this need not be the case – and invite our readers to consider how aesthetic judgements might legitimately inform appraisal of creative and expressive work in the arts. Our theoretical effort was made necessary because we found ourselves in difficulty when trying to formulate the art process in curriculum terms with our teacher collaborators. Most of the project's arts teachers readily described themselves as committed in principle to children's self-expression and personal development, but when pressed they seemed to have only hazy notions as to what this might mean as an overarching theory. Interestingly, Schön's account of 'artful enquiry' (the practice of reflection-in-action) in many ways echoes Witkin's (1974) description of the creative process in art.

Of all the four questions posed by Schön, that concerned with role-framing is particularly significant for our research. If many of our teachers seemed to flounder in the assessment conversation – and it must be remembered that most of the conversations we collected yielded almost nothing we could use to demonstrate what we had in mind, only yet more examples of what we were trying to get away from – it was to some degree due to the fact that what we were asking of them could not easily be encompassed within the technical-rational mode to which most of them wittingly or unwittingly subscribed. Put another way, real 'conversations' between teachers and pupils seemed out of the question, on institutional and professional grounds, even when enough time and suitable spaces could be found. Ben and Kenny, Stan and Karen, Michael and Fiona are all locked into relationships that seem to prohibit intimacy, playfulness, empathy, reciprocity. Ben, Stan and Michael stick to rigid agendas determined by largely safe technical considerations. None of them really listens to the pupil, really 'sees' the work under consideration. Only Frank and Susie achieve moments of spontaneity and surprise. For Malcolm on the other hand the situation could hardly have been more different. He was free to frame his relationship in very different terms. Granted he was a stranger to Louise, and as Jack's father might have experienced other difficulties in the conversation, but he was free to try to establish the ambience most suited to his objectives and experienced none of the tensions that so evidently inhibited the teachers. The implications for the assessment conversation are considerable, because the necessary conditions cannot easily be satisfied within the technical-rational paradigm.

Taking up the concerns our teachers expressed over traditional assessment in the arts, we now feel able to suggest ways forward. A pupil's self-esteem and confidence need not be at risk in a genuine conversation designed to support her own reflection and help her make informed and constructive judgements while at the same time hearing the opinions and advice of her partner. Grading in the arts must be criterion related and not based upon normative, positivistic structures. Whenever possible, grading should be accompanied by a rich descriptive profile of each student based upon what they are able to achieve in a supportive situation (Vygotsky 1972). A teacher's tastes and preferences need not unduly determine the final assessment of a piece of work. On the contrary, the question of personal response by both partners will help enrich the possibility of interpretation: the teacher's view will be respected for what it is rather than meekly acquiesced to. On the other hand, both partners will be aware that personal taste and preference are profoundly affected by – because they are rooted in – culturally authorized criteria for judging what is good and what is bad in art. Similarly, principles of individuality and singularity will be tempered by an appreciation of the social and cultural dimensions of authenticity. Authentic work in the arts achieves currency through social practices that subsume and transcend the person. As for comparison and competition, although these are intrinsic to the human condition they need not be merely baleful in their effect upon pupils. What has to be stressed is the pupil's perpetual struggle or competition with herself – to be more perceptive, more discerning, more articulate. Above all, we hope to have shown that a professional and responsible approach to the identification and tracking of impulse in creative, expressive work can yield valuable insights for both teacher and pupil, and can contribute significantly to a holistic, comprehensive assessment that pays proper regard to the primacy of feeling, of sensibility, in aesthetic understanding.

Focusing on talk as a medium of transaction and assessment, our research has exposed a largely unexplored area of experience for most arts teachers and their pupils. What we have called 'sensible' conversation in the aesthetic domain is a vast untapped resource. And look what talk can do! Such talk as is recorded in this book could on its own be a justification for according higher status to the arts in education. Since the term was first coined by Andrew Wilkinson in 1965, *oracy* has increasingly been recognized as an important dimension of learning. In talking about ideas and feelings with which they are closely involved – which are close to their hearts – pupils show great versatility in their use of spoken language: they entertain possibilities, doubts, make connections, tell stories, explain processes and motivations, state their case, express pleasure, reservation and conviction. In the right circumstances they respond warmly and socially, using talk both introspectively to make and explore sense and meaning, and, generously, as a way of sharing, conversing, communicating, validating, complying. The arts teachers we worked with on this project not infrequently expressed surprise at their pupils' verbal abilities. Were we teachers to become better conversationalists, developing greater attentiveness, a more vivid and engaged sense of the verbal interaction and of what it might become, then how much greater our grounds for surprise and for satisfaction might be. Within the school context the pupils themselves have little power to institute change. The onus is therefore on teachers to manage new opportunities for talk and to experiment with new forms and focuses of talking. Given a proper understanding of what talk can do to enhance a pupil's aesthetic development, the arts could move to the forefront of the campaign for recognition of the educational importance of talk as a medium of social engagement and shared learning. Not only has talk an important contribution to make to the arts, but equally, we would like to suggest, the arts have a valuable part to play in the promotion of spoken language as a cross-curricular skill.

This project has also discovered something important for assessment in the arts. It is a sort of general principle: pupils must first know *what* they have done before they are in any position to judge *how* they have done. This principle underlies the assessment conversation; the pupil and teacher as assessors must first recover and discover the imaginative object (image) as a real presence before attempting to assess competence, skills and understanding.

Looking back at our early interviews with teachers, we can now redefine their problems with assessment as stemming from a fundamental difficulty as to how to reconcile the so-called 'teachable' elements of the arts curriculum with what is essentially 'untaught': conventional forms and expressive materials transformed by subjective feelings. Having little concern for what Louis Arnaud Reid called 'embodied meaning', leaving little scope for a personal sense of form and feeling as an integrated whole – in other words, with an inadequately defined knowledge-base – a comprehensive, aesthetic assessment for our teachers was impossible. So they came across as uncertainly objective, apologetically subjective, and frequently as either radically blocking or simply ignoring the voice of the pupil. We hope to have contributed to assessment in the arts by re-articulating the knowledge-base in curricular terms. We are clearer now about what counts as learning in the arts: contemplation and reflection, praise and publication take their place alongside process and production, technique and practicality. The customary imbalance is redressed and there is cause for confidence in a comprehensive assessment that allows to subjectivity its central role in aesthetic experience, and sees the making and enjoyment of art works as complementary aspects of arts education.

Late on in our research our own confidence was boosted when we found our process model for an integrated arts curriculum mirrored in and, in a sense, vindicated by the theoretical position of the gestalt school of counselling[5]. To us, our model closely matches the 'cycle of formation and destruction' that provides the theoretical framework for gestalt counselling practice (see Figure 4).

Clarkson's (1989) account of the 'last contact' and 'satisfaction' stages replicates in many respects our descriptions of praise and publication. Of satisfaction, Clarkson observes:

> This post-contact or satisfaction phase is frequently omitted from theoretical discussions of the cycle. This may be a reflection of the lack of importance sometimes accorded to the closing phases of human experiences . . . It is common for people to worry about events for long periods before they

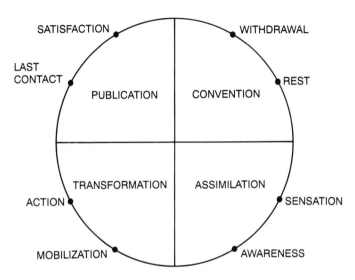

Figure 4 The gestalt cycle superimposed upon our own arts model. *Source*: Gestalt cycle adapted from Clarkson (1989).

happen; it is less usual for people to celebrate events for long periods after they have happened . . . This period of gradual assimilation, of 'coming down', of savouring experiences as they are receding from focus and fading into the background can be the source of deep pleasure or profound learning.

(Clarkson 1989)

The neglect of *celebration* that Clarkson identifies here seems to correspond with our own sense that creative appraisal – contemplation and reflection – are both undervalued and under-utilized by teachers of the arts. Once recognized, however, the phase of 'savouring', of celebration, can be a profoundly satisfying aspect of the whole creative cycle, at the moment of letting go.

Hitherto the arts have all too often been assessed from an external point of view as products. It is our belief that for the arts such assessment is neither sufficient nor satisfactory since it avoids that which is most to be valued in arts learning: the subjective *making of aesthetic meaning*. If we are to assess this central mode of experiencing we must start elsewhere than the disembodied product and the public, impositional, normative domain. We must start with the pupil's act of publication. This act of publication has, to a considerable degree, been the focus of our project. We have shown it to be a rich, many-faceted, social encounter that makes special use of conversational talk and calls for a particular quality of relationship between pupil and teacher. If there is a lesson to be learnt from the project it is just how radical and profound is the programme of self-reappraisal and professional realignment that arts teachers may need to commit themselves to.

Assessment in education traditionally has the kiss of death about it, and not just where the arts are concerned: the assessment-led English National Curriculum is already in difficulty. For many children assessment means enduring a form of mental and emotional derangement, the morbid exchange of a warm, living experience for a cold, dead reckoning. Accountability in education has to be rescued from the accountants – mere reckoning must make way for the lively exchange of human insight and intuition. The experiences documented in this book suggest the possibility of a radically new account of assessment in arts education. Again, by chance, we have happened at the very end of the project upon precisely the concept we have been looking for, unknowingly, to encapsulate the liberating, self-affirming, celebratory experience that has been our most rewarding discovery. Assessment in the arts can provide the pupil with an experience uniquely freeing and empowering – if we adhere to the notion that judgements in the arts must be and must always remain 'suspended judgements'. This is an idea propounded by the British novelist and poet John Cowper Powys (1975) in a collection of essays to which he gave this title. For Powys, the heart of criticism is that process by which the individual sinks into her/his own soul and finds in feeling a unique habitation. Judgement in the arts must be 'guarded from the impertinence of judicial decision by its confessed implication of *radical subjectivity*' (our emphasis). We have only broached this idea, but it seems to us to be profoundly rich and important. In such moments of shared and privileged reflection, assessment as a creative dimension of an unending cycle of self-discovery and regeneration comes fully into its own. 'When a practitioner becomes a researcher into his own practice, he engages in a continuing process of self-education' (Schön 1983: 299).

It is often said these days that realistic teaching means teaching only that which can be properly assessed. Our experience suggests, regrettably, that in the absence of an appropriate assessment practice this may be all too true of creative and expressive work in the arts. We hope that in proposing a fresh approach to assessment we may prompt a renewed interest in teaching for the development of aesthetic understanding.

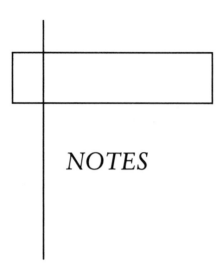

NOTES

1 By this stage we had come to understand the purpose of the assessment conversation as generating or being characterized by what Witkin (1974) called the 'intelligence of feeling'.

2 Michael Oakeshott's 'The voice of poetry in the conversation of mankind' was a seminal influence upon the present project's thinking. We are grateful to Martin Golding for bringing it to our notice.

3 The English painter J.M.W. Turner (1775–1851) painted a picture entitled 'Dawn After the Wreck' in which the same connotative problem is addressed. Turner cheats somewhat by depicting a half-drowned dog howling on the otherwise deserted beach.

4 As so often with our project, we experienced a lucky break just when we needed it. In this case it was Margaret Barrett (University of Tasmania) who reminded us of the literature on 'reflection'.

5 We are grateful to Margot Sutherland, Director of the Institute for Arts in Therapy and Education (Regent's College, London), for pointing us to the Clantson model.

REFERENCES AND
BIBLIOGRAPHY

Barnes, D. (1976) *From Communication to Curriculum*. Harmondsworth: Penguin.

Barthes, R. (1970) *The Responsibility of Forms*. Oxford: Basil Blackwell.

Boud, D., Keogh, R. and Walker, D. (1985) *Reflection: Turning Experience into Learning*. London: Kogan Page.

Broadfoot, P. (1979) *Assessment, Schools and Society*. London: Methuen.

Broadfoot, P. (ed.) (1984) *Selection, Certification and Control*. Lewes: Falmer Press.

Broadfoot, P., Murphy, R. and Torrance, H. (eds) (1990) *Changing Educational Assessment*. London: Routledge and Kegan Paul.

Brown, S. (1990) Assessment: a changing practice. In T. Horton (ed.) *Assessment Debates*. London: Hodder and Stoughton.

Bruner, J. (1966) *Towards a Theory of Instruction*. Cambridge, MA: MIT Press.

Carr, W. and Kemmis, S. (1986) *Becoming Critical*. Lewes: Falmer Press.

Clarkson, P. (1989) *Gestalt Counselling in Action*. London: Sage.

DES (1985) *Better Schools*. London: HMSO.

Frederikson, J. and Collins, A. (1989) A systems approach to educational testing, *Educational Researcher* 18(9): 27–32.

Harré, R. (1983) *Personal Being*. Oxford: Basil Blackwell.

Hargreaves, D. (1982) *The Challenge of the Comprehensive School*. London: Routledge and Kegan Paul.

Kelly, G. A. (1955) *The Psychology of Personal Constructs, volumes 1 and 2.* New York: Norton.

Langer, S. (1953) *Feeling and Form.* London: Routledge and Kegan Paul.

Macintosh, H. (1988) 'Some observations on TGAT'. Unpublished paper presented at Nuffield Assessment Seminar Group.

Mitchell, P. (1989) The professional teacher's role in assessment, *Forum* 31(1): 7–9.

National Oracy Project (1991) *Assessment through Talk in Key Stages 3 & 4 and Beyond.* London: NCC Enterprises.

Nuttall, D. (1991) 'Assessment developments in the USA'. Unpublished paper presented at BERA Annual Conference.

Oakeshott, M. (1977) *Rationalism in Politics and Other Essays.* London: Methuen.

Osbourn, R. J. (1988) 'The aesthetic response: an application of personal construct theory to the perception and appraisal of visual art, volumes 1 and 2'. Unpublished PhD thesis, University of Exeter.

Paris, S., Lawton, T. A., Turner, J. C. and Roth, J. L. (1991) A developmental perspective on standardized achievement testing, *Educational Researcher* 20(5): 12–20.

Perry, L. (1984) The arts, judgment and language, *Journal of Aesthetic Education* 18(1): 21–33.

Powys, J. C. (1975) *Suspended Judgements.* London: Village Press.

Reid, L. A. (1969) *Meaning in the Arts.* London: Allen and Unwin.

Roach, J. (1971) *Public Examinations in England 1850–1900.* Cambridge: Cambridge University Press.

Ross, M. (1991) The hidden order of arts education, *The British Journal of Aesthetics* 31(2): 111–21.

Rowntree, D. (1977) *Assessing Students: How Shall We Know Them?* London: Harper and Row.

Sapir, E. (1949) *Selected Writings in Language, Culture and Personality.* Berkeley: University of California Press.

Schön, D. A. (1983) *The Reflective Practitioner: How Professionals Think in Action.* Aldershot: Avebury.

SEAC (1991) *Teacher Assessment at Key Stage 3.* London: HMSO.

Siegel, H. (1988) *Educating Reason.* London: Routledge.

Steiner, G. (1989) *Real Presences: Is There Anything* in *What We Say?* London: Faber and Faber.

Stevens, W. (1955) *The Collected Poems of Wallace Stevens.* London: Faber.

TGAT (1988) *Task Group on Assessment and Testing, a Report.* London: DES.

Torrance, H. (1989) Theory, practice and politics in the development of assessment, *Cambridge Journal of Education* 19(2): 183–91.

Tyler, R. (1986) Changing concepts of educational evaluation, *International Journal of Educational Research* 10(1): 11–19.

Vygotsky, L.S. (1972) *Thought and Language*. Cambridge, MA: MIT Press.

Waller, W. (1932) *The Sociology of Teaching*. Chichester: John Wiley and Sons (1967 edition).

Wilkinson, A.M. (1965) with contributions by A. Davies and D. Atkinson. 'Spoken English, educational review', Occasional Paper No. 2, University of Birmingham School of Education.

Winnicott, D.W. (1971) *Playing and Reality*. London: Tavistock.

Witkin, R.W. (1974) *The Intelligence of Feeling*. London: Heinemann Educational.

Wolf, D. (1988) Opening up assessment, *Educational Leadership* 45(4): 24–29.

Wood, R. (1987) *Measurement and Assessment in Education and Psychology*. Lewes: Falmer Press.

Woolf, V. (1966) *Collected Essays, volume 2*. Toronto: Hogarth Press.

INDEX

accountability, 10, 11, 168
aesthetic, 46, 48, 50
  contemplation, 28, 34, 35, 38,
    52, 56, 58, 61, 64, 69, 102,
    120, 160
  criteria, 81, 158
  development, 6, 15, 17, 38, 41,
    50, 52, 63
  education, 4, 15, 158
  experience, 9, 28, 40, 50,
    159
  interpretation, 56, 81, 85
  judgement, 9, 12, 23, 36, 38,
    39, 41, 51, 54, 56, 64, 70,
    161, 163, 164, 168
  knowing, 36, 50, 53, 57, 58,
    59, 125, 161
  meaning, 15, 62, 119, 167
  non-, 57, 58, 59, 60, 86
  perception, 50, 58, 69, 125
  reception, 140, 142
  reflection, 28, 35
  response, 41, 50, 57, 58, 59,
    60, 61, 63, 64, 86, 141
  understanding(s), 10, 17, 23,
    34, 37, 38, 39, 46, 50, 52,
    54, 55, 57, 61–6, 69, 70, 99,
    100, 154, 165, 169
America (USA), 15, 16
affect, 9, 22, 41, 141, 150
appropriation, 51–66, 70, 75, 89,
  92, 94, 115, 140
art
  composition, 46, 81, 136
  content, 136, 147, 150
  context, 39, 150
  design (and), 7, 8
  discourse, 33, 54
  inspiration, 46, 53, 110, 144
  making, 22, 34, 38, 47, 73, 75,
    115, 120, 135, 158, 160
  meaning, 34, 35
  object, 92, 117
  practice, 79, 104

process, 20, 35, 73, 80, 109
product, 9, 20, 27, 28, 30, 51,
  52, 69, 75, 92, 109, 147,
  167
school, 8, 161, 162
skills, 24, 30
technical dimension, 34, 73, 76,
  78, 90, 93, 104, 105, 108,
  149
artefact, 9, 28, 51
arts
  achievement in the, 10, 17, 168
  assessment in the, 7, 9, 16,
    158, 159
  curriculum the, 8, 10, 35, 41,
    47, 50–66, 158, 166
  experience, 18, 23
  in education, 4, 6, 7, 16, 17,
    28, 34, 52, 57, 158, 166
  knowledge base of the, 7–9
  media, 9, 38
  teaching methods in the, 7, 24
assessment
  achievement (of), 15, 17
  appraisal, 37, 78, 131, 158
  celebration, as, 56, 161
  contemplation, 38, 46
  conversation, 26, 27, 34–38,
    56, 69, 99, 159,
    163–5
  criteria, 9, 11, 17, 163
  criterion-referenced, 10, 164
  descriptive, 16, 164
  evidence, 36, 41, 46, 55, 66,
    70, 87, 100, 104, 157
  formative, 13–15, 17, 24, 25,
    27, 29, 47, 56, 131, 141,
    143, 161
  grades, 9, 10, 16, 164
  information, 12, 38
  judgement(s), 12, 38, 46, 66,
    142, 156, 168
  marks, 16, 24
  models of, 9, 11

national, 11, 15
National Curriculum in the, 11,
  14
norm-referenced, 10, 158, 163,
  164, 168
profile, 13, 52, 164
qualitative, 15, 16, 38, 41
quantitative, 15, 20, 48
reflective, 16, 17, 38, 156
reporting, 10, 24, 157
selection, 12, 14
self-assessment, 16, 17, 25, 36,
  37, 99, 131, 135, 158
standardized, 11, 16
strategy, 10, 12, 14, 26
summative, 13–15, 24, 25, 38,
  73, 81, 143, 157
talk (through), 17, 25, 26,
  61–6, 131, 144, 164, 165
Task Group on, 11, 14, 15
teacher, 13, 14, 15, 55
traditional, 58, 164, 168
validation, 35, 56, 140, 141,
  143
verdict, 36, 46
verification, 36, 38
attainment target(s), 5, 160
attention, 38, 39, 57, 58, 61, 63,
  73, 79, 122, 131, 138, 144,
  149, 154
audience, 56, 133–5, 141–5
authenticity, 18, 35, 37, 39, 53,
  122, 141, 148, 151, 164

Barnes, D., 17, 22, 23
Broadfoot, P., 11, 12
Brown, Sally, 14, 15
bureaucracy, 17, 161, 162

Callaghan, James, 1, 6
celebration, 161, 167, 168
Clarkson, P., 166, 167
cognition, 9, 50, 63
commitment, 25, 45

composition, 46, 81, 136
conventionalization, 51–66, 70,
    72, 75, 81, 89, 98, 100, 109,
    130, 141, 148, 151
connation, 63, 95, 102, 150
contemplation, 28, 34, 35, 38,
    46, 52, 56, 58, 61, 63, 64,
    69, 102, 120, 160
convention, 76, 79
conversation, 17, 18, 26, 27, 34,
    35, 37–48, 53, 59–66, 82,
    90, 143, 163–5
    partner, 60, 65, 144, 161, 164
creativity, 3, 8, 9, 10, 17, 20, 21,
    24, 26, 34, 36, 46, 47, 51,
    56, 71, 96, 143, 144, 158,
    161, 169
culture, 23, 53, 164
cultural context, 39, 54
curriculum
    arts, 8, 10, 35, 41, 47, 50–66,
    158, 166
    assessment of the, 2, 6, 11
    delivery of the, 4, 160
    National Curriculum, 1, 3, 4,
    7, 8, 10, 11, 13, 14, 18, 48,
    91, 160, 168
    objectives, 10, 21

dance, 4, 7, 66, 130–45, 162
'depth' dimension, 62–6, 75, 85,
    89, 91, 109, 112, 122, 123,
    125, 126, 133, 138, 147
Department of Education and
    Science (DES), 6, 11
dialectic, 136, 151, 152
drama, 4, 7, 8, 22, 23, 100–5,
    162

education
    aesthetic, 4, 15, 158
    arts, 4, 6, 7, 16, 17, 28, 34,
    52, 57, 158, 166
    Reform Act, 7, 11

emotion, 141, 154
English, 3, 4, 6, 90–100
examinations, 10, 11
    results, 3, 24
expression, 8–10, 20, 24–6, 33,
    36, 39, 46, 48, 51, 53–6, 58,
    73, 82, 96, 147, 158, 161,
    163, 169

feeling, 9, 17, 34, 36, 37, 40,
    53–5, 57, 61, 63, 82, 86, 89,
    94, 97, 100, 102, 104, 123,
    135, 140, 141, 147, 150,
    153, 155, 165
    feeling impulse, 33, 35, 38, 54,
    62, 76, 78, 98, 147
    form, 61, 104, 112, 126, 153
    intelligence, 55, 59, 70
form, 9, 36, 38, 61, 89, 94, 104,
    123, 140, 141, 153, 154
formal elements, 91, 93, 100, 138

General Certificate of Secondary
    Education (GCSE), 10, 11,
    25, 100, 105, 108, 130, 163
gestalt, 39, 152
    counselling, 161
gesture, 136, 137

Harré, Rom, 50, 52
holding form, 39, 123, 136

identity project(s), 51, 53, 54
image, 36, 38, 46, 54, 73, 85, 90,
    117, 150, 166
imagery, 55, 133
imagination, 8, 25, 35, 36, 63,
    71, 78, 82, 86, 97, 98, 100,
    115, 117, 126, 133, 140,
    145, 154, 155, 158
imaginative significance, 62, 63,
    65
improvisation, 42, 135, 145
individuality, 16, 17